LONDON
POCKET ATLAS & GUIDE

(GEOGRAPHIA)

ROBERT NICHOLSON PUBLICATIONS

First published 1981

2nd edition 1984

© Text, **Robert Nicholson Publications Limited 1984**

Central London and London Maps
© **Geographia Limited**
based upon the Ordnance Survey with the sanction of the
controller of Her Majesty's Stationery Office.
Crown Copyright reserved.

London Underground map by
kind permission of London Transport.
Registered User Number 84/067

All other maps
© Robert Nicholson Publications Limited

Robert Nicholson Publications Limited
17–21 Conway Street
London W1P 6JD

Great care has been taken throughout this book to be accurate,
but the publishers cannot accept responsibility for any errors
which appear or their consequences.

Typeset by Book Economy Services
Cuckfield Sussex

Printed in the United Kingdom by
Blantyre Printing & Binding Company Limited
Blantyre, Glasgow

First, some basic information about money. For cash, banks offer the best rate of exchange (*open 09.30–15.30 Mon to Fri, closed Bank hols*). Some department stores have bureaux de change, most hotels will cash traveller's cheques.

London Guide 1

GETTING ABOUT

TOURIST INFORMATION
City of London Information Centre   B43
St Paul's Churchyard EC4. 01-606 3030. All about the City. *Diary of Events* lists free entertainment.

National Tourist Information Centre   A59
Main forecourt, Victoria Station SW1. Multi-lingual tourist and travel information. Also instant hotel reservations, theatre and tour bookings. Bookshop. *Open 09.00–20.30, 08.30–22.00 Jul & Aug.* Telephone information service: 01-730 3488.

Harrods, Knightsbridge SW1	B48
Heathrow Central Underground Station	
Selfridges, Oxford St W1	B38
Tower of London, West Gate E1	A55

TRAVEL
Underground trains and buses usually stop between *24.00 and 06.00*. However, there are some all-night buses and if you are planning a late night out in town, consult 'The Night Owl's Guide' available from London Transport Information Centre or telephone 01-222 1234 at any time. All underground stations have a notice of first and last trains. Some bus stops list first and last buses.

London Transport Travel Information Centres
For enquiries on tube and bus travel, sight-seeing tours and special cut-price touring tickets:

Euston Underground Station	B33
Heathrow Central Underground Station	
King's Cross Underground Station	A34
Oxford Circus Underground Station	B40
Piccadilly Circus Underground Station	A50
Victoria Underground Station	A59

ENTERTAINMENT FOR FREE

How to spend a pleasant hour or so without spending money. Here are some famous London attractions.

CHANGING OF THE GUARD

Telephone London Tourist Board (01-730 3488) for details.

Buckingham Palace   B49

SW1. New guard marches from Chelsea or Wellington Barracks; changes *11.30 daily, alt days in winter*.

Horseguards Parade   B51

Whitehall SW1. Queen's Life Guard, on great black horses, leave Hyde Park Barracks *10.38 Mon-Sat, 09.39 Sun*. Ceremony *11.00 Mon-Sat, 10.00 Sun*.

CHURCH CONCERTS

Free lunchtime concerts, though there is usually a collection.

St Bride   B42

Fleet St EC4. 01-353 1301. *Wed*.

St Martin-in-the-Fields   A51

Trafalgar Sq WC2. 01-930 0089. *Mon & Tue*.

St John's   A61

Smith Square SW1. 01-222 1061. *Mon & alt Thur*.

HOUSES OF PARLIAMENT   A61

St Margaret St SW1. 01-219 3000. Look around the Victorian-Gothic pile (built 1840–68 by Sir Charles Barry and A. W. N. Pugin) when Parliament is in recess. Or queue for admission during debates. Be sure to admire the famous clock tower (Big Ben is the name of the bell inside).

MILITARY AND BRASS BANDS

For rousing British music go to a public park on a summer afternoon. Check *What's On & Where to Go* for details. Try:

Lincoln's Inn Fields   B42

WC2. *Tue lunchtime*.

St James's Park   B50

SW1. *Every lunchtime and early eve*.

Regent's Park   A32

NW1. *Every lunchtime and early eve*.

OLD BAILEY   B43

Old Bailey EC4. 01-248 3277. Climb to the public gallery to watch criminals getting their come-uppance. *Mon-Fri*.

SPEAKER'S CORNER   A48

Marble Arch corner of Hyde Park. Where unknown orators explain their views of life. Feel free to argue. *Sun*.

SEEING THE SIGHTS

Apart from the cost of getting there, seeing the sights is also free. Here are some of the most dramatic, most intriguing and most British of them.

Buckingham Palace   **B49**
St James's Pk SW1. London residence of the Sovereign (the Royal Standard flies when she is at home). Built 1705, remodelled by Nash 1825, refaced by Sir Ashton Webb 1913.

The Cenotaph   **B51**
Whitehall SW1. Designed 1920 by Sir Edward Lutyens to honour the dead of World War I. Wreaths are laid here annually at the culmination of the Remembrance Day Service in memory of those who fell in both world wars.

City of London   **B44**
The 'square mile' of the City is the oldest part of London and the centre of banking, insurance and stockbroking. Look for sections of the Roman Wall, medieval streets and alleys, old taverns and churches that survived the Great Fire of 1666.

Covent Garden   **B41**
The former home of the famous fruit and vegetable market – today one of London's most popular meeting places. Grand Victorian warehouses shelter craft shops, gift stalls, wine bars, restaurants and art galleries. Originally designed by Inigo Jones in the 1630s.

Downing St   **B51**
17thC houses built by Sir George Downing. No 10 is the official residence of the Prime Minister, No 11 of the Chancellor of the Exchequer. Handy for the Houses of Parliament, the offices and Ministries of Whitehall.

Fleet St   **B42**
The street of communications and the law. Many national newspapers have their offices on or just off it. Watch the legal eagles at work and play.

Piccadilly Circus   **B40**
Six major streets meet at the fountain and statue of Eros (Gilbert 1892). Not the glamorous meeting place it once was, but its fame lingers on. The young crowd permanently camped around the statue is still very much of today.

St Paul's Cathedral   **B43**
EC4. 01-248 4619/2705. Built by Christopher Wren from 1675–1710, and considered his greatest work. Superb dome, porches and monuments. The setting in 1981 for the marriage of Charles, Prince of Wales and Lady Diana Spencer.

Soho   **B40**
London's oldest 'foreign quarter', encompassing the whole of Chinatown. Plenty of foreign restaurants, also plenty of sex in the form of strip shows, blue movies, 'young models' and sex aid shops for DIY enthusiasts.

The Temple   A52
Inner Temple, Crown Office Row EC4. 01-353 8462. Middle
Temple, Middle Temple La EC4. 01-353 4355. Two Inns of Court.
Wander round the courtyards, alleys, gardens and the early Gothic
'round' church built by the Templars. *At weekends & B. hols enter
via Embankment.*

Trafalgar Square   A51
Nelson's column (1840) guarded by Landseer's bronze lions.
Meeting place for political demonstrators and pigeons.

Westminster Abbey   A61
(The Collegiate Church of St Peter in Westminster) Broad
Sanctuary SW1. 01-222 5152. Original church by Edward the
Confessor, 1065. Rebuilt by Henry III from 1245 and completed
1376–1506. Fine perpendicular with fan vaulting. Contains
Coronation Chair, tombs and memorials of the Royalty of England
and their subjects.

MUSEUMS AND GALLERIES

When it rains, here are some interesting and stimulating shelters,
all free unless otherwise indicated.

British Museum   A41
Gt Russell St WC1. 01-636 1555. One of the largest and greatest in
the world – Egyptian mummies, Assyrian bulls, Elgin Marbles,
Rosetta Stone. *Closed Sun morn.*

Hayward Gallery   B52
Belvedere Rd SE1. 01-928 3144. Riverside gallery housing major
art exhibitions, which change regularly. *Closed Sun morn.
Admission charge.*

Imperial War Museum   A62
Lambeth Rd SE1. 01-735 8922. National collection on all aspects
of war since 1914, contained in an ex-lunatic asylum. *Closed Sun
morn.*

Madame Tussauds   A38
Marylebone Rd NW1. 01-935 6861. Waxen images of the famous
and notorious, life-size and life-like. Chamber of Horrors gets the
adrenalin going. *Admission charge.*

Museum of London   A43
London Wall EC2. 01–600 3699. A 3-dimensional biography of the
City and London area. *Closed Sun morn and Mon.*

National Gallery   A51
Trafalgar Sq WC2. 01-839 3321. Built 1838 by W. Wilkins and
containing a fine representative collection of the various schools of
painting. *Closed Sun morn.*

Natural History Museum   A57
Cromwell Rd SW7. 01-589 6323. Exhibitions of zoology, entomo-
logy, palaeontology and botany. *Closed Sun morn.*

Planetarium A38
Marylebone Rd NW1. 01-486 1121. Beginner's guide to the galaxy. The universe is represented hourly on the domed ceiling, with a commentary. *Admission charge.*

Science Museum A57
Exhibition Rd SW7. 01-589 3456. Large collection of working models and special exhibitions on the history of science and its application to industry. *Closed Sun morn.*

Tate Gallery B61
Millbank SW1. 01-821 1313. Famous for its representative collections of British paintings from the 16thC to the present day; also rich in foreign paintings and British and European sculpture. *Closed Sun morn.*

Victoria and Albert Museum A57
Cromwell Rd SW7. 01-589 6371. Vast collection of decorative art from all categories, countries and ages. Over 10 acres of museum! *Closed Sun morn and all Fri.*

Wallace Collection B38
Hertford House, Manchester Sq W1. 01-935 0687. Fine private collection of paintings, furniture, porcelain and armour, bequeathed to the nation by Lady Wallace in 1897. *Closed Sun morn.*

WHEN THE SUN SHINES

Sunny days call for open spaces, water and trees. Try:

Hampstead Heath, NW3
01-340 5603. 790 acres of parkland, sandy hills and wooded valleys. Once haunted by highwaymen, now crowded with visitors to the Bank Holiday fairs and famous inns – The Bull & Bush, Spaniard's and Jack Straw's Castle. Superb views. Also, wander through the streets of Hampstead – famous for its literary and artistic connections, as well as its appealing 'village' atmosphere.

Hyde Park, W1 A47
01-262 5484. 340 acres of Royal parkland with Rotten Row for horse riders, the Serpentine for fishermen, boaters, swimmers and admirers of ducks, and an open-air bar and restaurant for the hungry or thirsty.

Jason's Trip
Opp 60 Blomfield Rd W9. 01-286 4328. Traditional narrow boats make 1½ hour return trips through Regent's Park Zoo to Hampstead Road Locks.

Kensington Gardens, W8 A46
01-937 4848. An elegant addition to Hyde Park, containing Kensington Palace, the peaceful sunken garden, Round Pond, Albert Memorial – and Peter Pan's statue!

Kenwood House
Hampstead La NW3. 01-348 1286. 18thC Robert Adam House,

with fine art collection and superb grounds. On Sat in summer, leading orchestras give lakeside concerts. Take a picnic. Book for tickets on 01-633 1707.

The London Zoo A32
Regent's Pk NW1. 01-722 3333. By Decimus Burton, 1827. Since then, famous architects have designed new quarters for one of the largest animal collections in the world. First class children's zoo. *Admission charge.*

Regent's Park Open Air Theatre B31
Inner Circle, Regent's Pk NW1. 01-486 2431. Round off a fine day by watching a play, usually Shakespearean, in an attractive outdoor setting. *May–Aug.*

St James's Park & Green Park, SW1
01-262 5484. The oldest Royal park with a Chinese-style lake, bridge and weeping willows. Richly populated bird sanctuary on Duck Island presided over by the magnificent pelicans.

TAKING TO THE RIVER

Good way to see London when the weather is fine. You can telephone the special River Boat Information Service on 01-730 4812. Below are two of the best trips.

GREENWICH

Westminster Pier B51
Victoria Embankment SW1. 01-930 4097. Boats leave for Greenwich about *every 40 min.*

The 'Cutty Sark'
King William Wlk SE10. 01-858 3445. While at Greenwich, see one of the great sailing tea clippers. *Admission charge.*

National Maritime Museum
Romney Rd SE10. 01-858 4422. Finest maritime collection in Britain. Incorporates Queen's House by Inigo Jones, 1616, and the Old Royal Observatory with its astronomical instruments and Planetarium. *Closed Mon.*

Royal Naval College
Greenwich SE10. 01-858 2154. Fine group of classical buildings by Webb, Wren and Vanburgh, fronting on to the river. Chapel by James Stuart, Painted Hall by Thornhill. *Closed Thur.*

KEW

Boats leave Westminster Pier for Kew *about every 30 min.*

Royal Botanic Gardens
Kew Rd, Surrey. 01-940 1171. One of the world's great botanic gardens with magnificent Victorian planthouses. 300 acres of green peace and unusual flowers. *Small charge.*

CULTURAL ENTERTAINMENT

For music, opera, ballet or theatre it is wise to book seats in advance at the Box Office (a Ticket Agency will charge commission). If you can face possible disappointment, try for 'returns' just before the performance. Brief details and times appear in *The Standard*, *What's On & Where To Go* and the national newspapers.

MUSIC

Royal Albert Hall   B46
Kensington Gore SW7. 01-589 8212. Huge, Victorian domed hall famous for the 'Proms'. Mainly orchestral and choral, but also pop concerts and meetings.

Royal Festival Hall   A52
South Bank SE1. 01-928 3191. Built 1951 as part of South Bank Arts Centre. Orchestral and choral concerts here, or in adjacent Queen Elizabeth Hall and Purcell Room.

St John's   A61
Smith Sq SW1. 01-222 1061. Solo recitals, chamber, orchestral and choral works in a unique 18thC church. Licensed buffet and art exhibitions in the crypt.

Wigmore Hall   B39
36 Wigmore St W1. 01-935 2141. By tradition, visiting musicians make their London debut in its intimate atmosphere. Chiefly chamber music and solo recitals.

OPERA AND BALLET

Coliseum   A51
St Martin's La WC2. 01-836 3161. Opera in English from the English National Opera (and from visiting companies). Also ballet performed for audiences of up to 2,400.

Royal Opera House, Covent Garden   B41
Bow St WC2. 01-240 1066. 24-hr information and bookings 01-240 1911. Where to see the world-famous Royal Opera and Royal Ballet companies. Those in the expensive seats often dress up for the occasion.

Sadler's Wells   B35
Rosebery Av EC1. 01-837 1672. The original well discovered by Thomas Sadler is under a trap-door at the back of the stalls. Birthplace of the Royal Ballet Company; now used by visiting opera and dance companies.

THEATRE

London has had live theatre for seven centuries. Today the greatest concentration of theatres is along, or just off, Shaftesbury Ave, Leicester Sq and within the Covent Garden area. See 'Theatres & Cinemas Map' on page 26.

Barbican (RSC) AA3
Barbican Centre, Barbican EC2. 01-628 8795. Purpose-built for the Royal Shakespeare Company. A large theatre for large scale productions and The Pit for the performance of work by new British playwrights. See the Master, revivals and classics.

Criterion A50
Piccadilly Circus W1. 01-930 3216. A listed building with preserved interior. Shows light comedies and straight drama.

Haymarket (Theatre Royal) A50
Haymarket SW1. 01-930 9832. Originally built in 1720 as 'The Little Theatre in the Hay'. Present theatre was designed by Nash in 1821. Stages light plays.

Lyric B40
Shaftesbury Av W1. 01-437 3686. Oldest theatre in Shaftesbury Av, built in 1888. Sarah Bernhardt performed here. Today, mainly plays and musicals.

National Theatre A52
South Bank SE1. 01-928 2252. The large apron-staged Olivier, smaller Lyttelton, and adaptable Cottesloe are the home of the National Theatre Company and stage a wide variety of plays. Daytime tours take you backstage and into the workshops.

Palladium B40
8 Argyll St W1. 01-437 7373. Houses top variety shows, the annual Royal Command Performance and a pantomime at Christmas.

Vaudeville A51
Strand WC2. 01-836 9988. Listed building. Originally ran farce and burlesque, then became straight; which for the most part it remains.

ROCK, POP AND ALL THAT JAZZ

For live music in a relaxed setting you can't beat the pubs and clubs. The charge is rarely high and membership, if necessary, is usually available at the door. For details see *What's On & Where to go*, or the music press.

Bull's Head
373 Lonsdale Rd SW13. 01-876 5241. Worth the trip south of the river to hear good modern jazz, every evening, from top English and visiting foreign players.

Golden Lion B57
490 Fulham Rd SW6. 01-385 3942. Music every evening, home-cooked lunches every day. Rock, blues, R & B.

Greyhound
175 Fulham Palace Rd W6. 01-385 0526. Famous old pub with interior purpose-built for staging music. Rock, punk and reggae.

Half Moon
93 Lower Richmond Rd, Putney, SW15. 01-788 2387. To the south again for this large pub with its spacious back room where

live music is played every night and on Sun lunchtime. Jazz, folk, rock, R & B.

Pindar of Wakefield   B34
328 Gray's Inn Rd WC1. 01-837 7269. And now for something completely different – traditional old-time music hall. Join in the choruses if you can. Food in a basket served while you watch. Essential to book.

Rock Garden   B41
6-7 The Piazza, Covent Garden WC2. 01-240 3961. American-style restaurant upstairs and on street level. Downstairs, nightly rock concerts (though never on *Sun*).

Ronnie Scott's   B40
46-49 Frith St W1. 01-439 0747. Enjoy the best jazz in London in a comfortable atmosphere with subtle lighting and good food. *Closed Sun. Admission charge.*

The Venue   A59
160-162 Victoria St SW1. 01-834 5500. Once a cinema, now a disco and rock joint with fast-food. Live bands play from *Mon-Sat to 02.00*. Check the press for details.

White Hart   B41
191 Drury La WC2. 01-405 4061. Good noisy jazz every evening – modern, trad and ragtime – in what is said to be the oldest pub in Covent Garden (with pubs, it's often hard to tell.)

STRICTLY FOR THE ENERGETIC

If the mixture of culture and night life is wearing you out, a bit of healthy exercise could work wonders.

SKATING PLACES
These are clubs, but you can join at the door. Pay by the hour and for skate hire. Tuition an optional extra.

Jubilee Hall   B41
Covent Garden Sq WC2. 01-836 2799. Regular roller skating and roller disco, run mainly by cheerful Australians. *Fri, Sat & Mon eve, Sun morn. Sat morn for under 16s, Sun afternoon for families.*

Queen's Ice Skating Club   B36
17 Queensway W2. 01-229 0172. If your wheels are running away with you, change to blades and cut a dash on the ice. Crowded and sociable with a licensed bar to help restore lost confidence.

SPORTS CENTRES
If you want to use the more popular facilities it is wise to book in advance.

Crystal Palace National Sports Centre
Crystal Palace SE19. 01-778 0131. Largest multi-sports centre in the country, right in Crystal Palace Park. Facilities include dry-

skiing, skating, squash, swimming. Fully equipped indoor sports hall. *Day membership scheme.*

YMCA: London Central A41
112 Gt Russell St WC1. 01-637 8131. Welcomes local and overseas members of both sexes. Indoor only, including gymnastics, swimming, table tennis and yoga. *Membership necessary.*

WALKING TOURS

A guided walk, usually with a special theme, is an inexpensive way of seeing more of London.

Mysterious Interiors of Hidden London A41
5 Bevan House, Boswell St WC1. 01-405 6191. A morning-long tour of the parts of London that even Londoners don't always reach. Starts from Holborn tube. *Tue–Thur 09.50.*

London Walks
139 Conway Rd, Southgate N14. 01-882 2763. Meet at various tube stations for walks (1½–2hrs) with titles like Legal and Illegal London, An Historic Pub Walk and The Famous Square Mile. *May–Oct, Mon—Fri eve.*

SINISTER LONDON

The older parts of London are somewhat grisly anyway, with their history of murder, martyrdom and ghosts. But if you relish the gruesome, try these extras.

Discovering London
11 Pennyfield, Worley, Brentwood, Essex. Brentwood 213704. Shuddery organised walks including Evil London, Night Prowl.

Highgate Cemetery
Swains La N6. 01-340 1834. Most graveyards have a certain creepy splendour – this one also has the dust of the famous, including Karl Marx, George Eliot and Faraday.

London Dungeon B54
34 Tooley St SE1. 01-403 0606. A horror museum in suitably unpleasant surroundings – huge damp vaults under London Bridge Station. Scenes of medieval torture garnished with stage blood. *Admission charge.*

Tower of London A55
Tower Hill EC3. 01-709 0765. Grim and famous fortress guarded by Beefeaters and ravens. See Traitors Gate (entrance of the doomed), armoury, executioner's block and axe – and the Crown Jewels. *Admission charge.*

Tower of Ramsgate A55
62 Wapping High St E1. 01-488 2685. At the end of an eerie day, restore the nerves with a drink in this 17thC riverside tavern, where, nearby, Colonel Blood was caught while trying to escape with the Crown Jewels. And below, pirates and smugglers used to be tied to be drowned by the incoming tide.

SHOPPING AROUND

London is immensely rich in shops, from large department stores to small specialists. The four main West End shopping streets are the very crowded Oxford St for department stores, clothes and shoes; the more sedate Regent St for expensive clothes, china and glass; Tottenham Court Rd for electronics and furniture; and Bond St for luxurious clothes, rugs, jewellery and pictures. *Most shops open 09.00–17.30 Mon–Sat.* Try:

Anything Left Handed   A50
65 Beak St W1. 01-437 3901. For the south-paws back home. More than 100 left-handed gadgets always in stock. *Closed Sat afternoons.*

Covent Garden General Store   B41
111 Long Acre. 01-240 0331. A large and bright store overflowing with gifts and novelties to solve every present problem. Basketware, bags, scarves, cosmetics, stationery and lots of gimmicky gift ideas. *Open to 24.00 Mon–Sat.*

The Design Centre   A50
28 Haymarket SW1. 01-839 8000. And now to raise the tone. Large showroom of the best in British design – all for sale to the discerning.

Fortnum and Mason   A50
181 Piccadilly W1. 01-734 8040. Elegant carpeted store selling luscious selection of unusual bottled and canned foods from all over the world. Worth admiring even if you can't afford to buy.

Foyles   B40
119–125 Charing Cross Rd WC2. 01-437 5660. The biggest of the bookshops. Aims to stock virtually every British book currently in print.

Harrods   B48
Knightsbridge SW1. 01-730 1234. Most famous of British department stores, laden with Royal Warrants. Massive food halls, huge range of clothes, books, animals (stuffed, skinned and living), banking hall, travel and booking agency – in fact, everything.

Hatchards   A50
187 Piccadilly W1. 01-439 9921. Good selection of general books and leather-bound editions.

HMV Record Store   B39
363 Oxford St W1. 01-629 1240. Probably the most comprehensive stock of records and cassettes in London.

Liberty's   B40
Regent St W1. 01-734 1234. Department store especially famous for its printed fabrics. Also particularly good on china, glass and fashion jewellery.

Marks & Spencer   A38 & B40
173 & 458 Oxford St W1. 01-734 4904/935 7954. Two major branches of this British shopping 'institution'. Good quality clothes for adults and children. You can't try things on but an exchange or refund is always forthcoming. Also food, books, etc.

Selfridges B40
400 Oxford St W1. 01-629 1234. Large and hectic department
store. Big food hall, huge household department; also clothes,
toys, furniture and sports gear. Garage parking.

GOING TO MARKET

Wholesale markets for serious business open around dawn. Small
markets for cheap fruit and veg, and 'antique' markets for bargains
and rip-offs, usually open shop hours. Here are 3 to look at and 3 to
shop in.

Berwick St B40
Soho W1. General market in the heart of Soho; fruit and vegetables
are good, prices reasonable. *Closed Sun*.

Billingsgate (wholesale)
North Quay, West India Docks Rd, Isle of Dogs. The new site of
London's principal fish market, moved from its age-old location in
the city. Still plenty of activity. Can be wet underfoot. *Open from
05.30 Tue–Sat*.

New Covent Garden (wholesale)
Nine Elms SW8. London's foremost wholesale fruit, vegetable and
flower market, moved from its Covent Garden site in 1974. *Open
from 04.00 Mon–Sat*.

Petticoat Lane B45
Radiates from Middlesex St E1. Huge bustling complex selling
everything under the sun; bargains, rubbish and fun. *Sun mornings
only*.

Portobello Road
Nr Notting Hill Gate tube W11. Famous flea market. Fruit, veg,
flowers, antiques, bizarre clothes and a welter of glorious junk. *Sat
only*.

Smithfield (wholesale) B43
Charterhouse St EC1. World's largest meat market. Interesting
architecture and storage techniques but for most people— 10 acres
of horror. *Open from 06.00 Mon–Fri*.

EATING AND DRINKING

FOOD
London can serve English and every kind of foreign food at all
prices. This brief selection is just to start you off. Most restaurants
open *12.00–15.00, 18.00–22.30*.

Fish and Chips
Almost a national dish in Britain. There are fish and chip shops all
over London, of varying quality. Some have tables, most do 'take-

away'; add salt and vinegar to taste and eat them from newspaper in traditional style.

Archduke A52
Concert Hall Approach SE1. 01-928 9370. Appealing wine bar built into a railway arch and abounding with brickwork, red pipes and hanging baskets. Plenty of wines; sausages are a speciality; French à la carte menu too. Live jazz and blues.

Cranks B40
8 Marshall St W1. 01-437 9431. One of the first wholefood vegetarian restaurants. Self-service, light, cheerful, popular. *Closes 20.30 Mon–Fri, 16.30 Sat & all Sun.*

Fawlty Towers B57
516–518 Fulham Rd SW6. 01-736 0240. Zany funhouse, where you can expect the unexpected. Dancing, cabaret and boisterous practical jokes. *Open to 01.00. Closed Sun.*

Flanagan's A38
100 Baker St W1. 01-935 0287. Phoney but enjoyable Victorian dining rooms. Cockney songs, singing waitresses, tripe, jellied eels, fish and chips and syrup pudding. Please don't spit in the sawdust!

Geale's Fish Restaurant
2–4 Farmer St W8. 01-727 7969. Informal restaurant with cheerful service. Good fish and real chips, crab soup, puddings, and wine by the glass. *Closed Sun & Mon.*

Hard Rock Café A49
150 Old Park La W1. 01-629 0382. Excellent hamburger joint with non-stop rock music. Long queues in evening.

Khan's
13 Westbourne Gro W2. 01-727 5420. Vast, bustling Indian restaurant with Oriental arches. Specialities include tandoori pot kebab, kofti dilruba and mutter paneer.

Lee Ho Fook B41
15 Gerrard St W1. 01-734 9578. In the heart of Chinatown and much-patronised by Chinese. Excellent cooking, generous portions, but service is slow. Famous for dim sum (steamed savouries in bamboo baskets).

Peppermint Park A51
13-14 Upper St Martin's La WC2. 01-836 5234. Crowded, lively atmosphere in this green and vivid pink restaurant. Cocktail bar and American food.

Tudor Rooms A51
80 St Martin's La WC2. 01-240 3978. Aptly termed a 'medieval theatre restaurant'. Five course olde English meal served by buxom wenches while troubadours, jesters and a dancing bear entertain. If you don't join in they actually put you in the stocks.

Vasco and Piero's Pavilion Restaurant B40
Academy Cinema, Poland St W1. 01-437 8774. Sample fine Italian cuisine accompanied by guitar music. Seafood salad, stinco arrosto, gâteau soaked in Grand Marnier. *Closed Sun.*

PUBS

The pub is uniquely English and many English pubs are unique. There are historical, literary, sporting and 'theme' pubs and London has more than 7,000. Here are 9 of the best. Usual hours *11.00-15.00, 17.30-23.00 Mon-Sat; 12.00-14.00, 19.00-22.30 Sun. (City pubs close early).*

Cheshire Cheese, Ye Olde   B42
145 Fleet St EC4. 01-353 6170. Rambling old building with low ceilings, oak tables and sawdusted floors above a 14thC crypt. Stout English food – famous for its winter game puddings. *Closes 20.30 and Sat & Sun.*

Cockney Pride   A50
6 Jermyn St SW1. 01-930 5339. Nostalgic reconstruction of a Victorian Cockney pub with traditional pub pianist and sausage and mash for the hungry.

George Inn   B53
77 Borough High St SE1. 01-407 2056. London's only remaining galleried coaching inn. From May to August, Southwark Arts Council puts on Shakespearean plays in the courtyard. Two bars, grill room and restaurant.

Lamb and Flag   A51
33 Rose St WC2. 01-836 4108. 300-year-old pub once known as 'The Bucket of Blood' when bare fist fights were held upstairs. Now a popular, mellow bar. Good lunchtime snacks and a noted real ale. Even more crowded than usual on Burns Night.

Mayflower
117 Rotherhithe St SE16. 01-237 4088. Tudor Inn originally called The Shippe, but renamed when the Mayflower, which set off from nearby, reached America. Licensed to sell English and US postage stamps. Nice restaurant.

Prospect of Whitby
57 Wapping Wall E1. 01-481 1095. Ancient dockland tavern dating back to Henry VIII's reign. Once used by so many thieves and smugglers they called it 'The Devils Tavern'. Restaurant with terrace overlooks the river.

St Stephen's Tavern   B51
10 Bridge St SW1. 01-930 3230. The MPs local – a bell rings to call them back to the House to vote. Restaurant with political cartoons – river views from the bar.

Samuel Pepys   A54
Brooks Wharf, 48 Upper Thames St EC4. 01-248 3691. Converted riverside warehouse. Light airy restaurant and cellar bar with food counter. Transcriptions of Pepys diaries, old lamps and prints. Also ticker-tape news from the wires of UNS and UPI.

Sherlock Holmes   A51
10 Northumberland St WC2. 01-930 2644. Upstairs, next to the restaurant, a reconstruction of the fictitious detective's study. Down in the bar, cuttings, curios and the head of The Hound of the Baskervilles!

Central London 2

Main Thoroughfares
with Bus Routes

Main Railway (B.R.) Stations

CHARING CROSS

Underground Railway Stations ⊖ Embankment

Principal Public Buildings

KING'S COLLEGE

Parks and Gardens

OXFORD STREET
Oxford Street, where specially marked, is closed
to through traffic (except buses and taxis)
between 7a.m. and 7p.m. Monday-Saturday

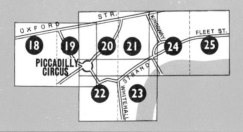

© GEOGRAPHIA LTD

*Based upon the Ordnance Survey Maps with
the sanction of the Controller of H.M. Stationery
Office.*

London Transport Underground Map Registered User Number 84/067

THE LONDON UNDERGROUND

○ Interchange with other Lines

⊖ Interchange with British Rail

[Fenchurch Street] Interchange with British Rail within walking distance

✦ Open Mondays to Fridays, peak hours only

★ Closed on Sundays

☆ Closed on Saturdays and Sundays

Certain stations are also closed on Public Holidays

🅱 Nearest stations for the Round London Sightseeing Tour

EUSTON Stations named in red have Travel Information Centres

▲ Piccadilly Line trains stop here early morning and late evening
Mondays to Saturdays and all day Sundays

RATHBONE PLA.

GT. TOTTENHM. CT. RD.

RUSSELL ST.

CONGRESS HO. (TUC)

DOMINION CINEMA

CLASSIC CINEMA

NEW OX

St GILES' CIRCUS

OXFORD STR.

Tottenham Ct. Rd.

ASTORIA CINEMA

ST. GILES HIGH ST.

SOHO

SUTTON ROW

DENMARK

ST. GILES IN THE FIELDS

COMPTON ST.

SQUARE

FILMCENTA 1,2 & 3

FRITH

GREEK

CHARING

PHOENIX THEA.

NEW

ABC CINEMAS 1 & 2

DEAN

PRINCE EDWARD

SEVE DIA.

WARDOUR

THE LONDONER CINEMA

PRINCE EDWARD

CAMB'DGE

EARLH M

AMBASSADORS THEA.

MONM

BERWICK ST.

OLD COMPTON ST.

R.

COLUMBIA CINEMA

CIRCUS PALACE THEA.

CROSS

WEST ST.

MARTIN'S TH.

ARTS THEA.

BREWER ST.

GLOBE THEA.

QUEEN'S THEA.

SHAFTESBURY

PR. CHARLES CINEMA

Leicester SQ.

GT NEWPT. ST.

APOLLO TH.

WINDMILL THD.MILL THEA.

LYRIC THEA.

WARDOUR ST.

RUPERT ST.

NEW EMPIRE RITZ CINEMA

LEICESTER ST.

LEIC. SQ.

WARNER CINE

WYNDHAM'S TH.

STR.

ST. MARTINS

MOULIN COMPLEX 1,2,3,4 & 5

PIGALLE

RIALTO CINE

SCENE 1,2,3 & 4

LEICESTER

CRANB'D

ODEON CINEMA

ALBERT THE

DUKE OF YORK'S TH.

EROS C PICCADILLY CIRCUS

LONDON PAVILION CINE

COVENTRY S.

AUTOMOBILE ASSOCN

SQ.

CLASSIC CINEMA

GARRICK THEA.

EROS

Piccadilly Circus

PR. OF WALES THEATRE

PANTON S.

IRVING ST.

CRITERION TH.

LEICESTER SQ. CINECENTA THEA.

COLISEUM
THEA

CHANDOS PL.

ADELPHI
THEA.

VAUDEVILLE
THEA.

SAVOY
THEA.

AGAR ST.

CARTING

LA.

WILLIAM IV. ST.

ST. MARTIN
IN THE
FIELDS

ROYAL SOCIETY
OF ARTS

JOHN ADAM ST.

S T R A N D

Embankment Gdns.

CLEOPATRA'S
NEEDLE

VILLIERS ST.

Charing Cross

SOUTH
AFRICA HO.

CHARING
CROSS

BAND
STAND

E M B A N K M E N T

JACEY
CIN.

CRAVEN STR.

Embankment

T H A M E S

RTHUMBERLAND AV.

HUNGERFORD BRI

Gt
SCOTLAND YD.

WHITEHALL PLA.

PS.
TATTERSHALL
CASTLE

OLD
WAR
OFFICE

WHITEHALL CT.

Gardens

V I C T O R I A

R I V E R

HORSEGUARDS AV.

W H I T E H A L L

MIN.OF
DEFENCE

MIN.OF
TECHNOLOGY

THE
CENOTAPH

LONDON
COUNTY HALL

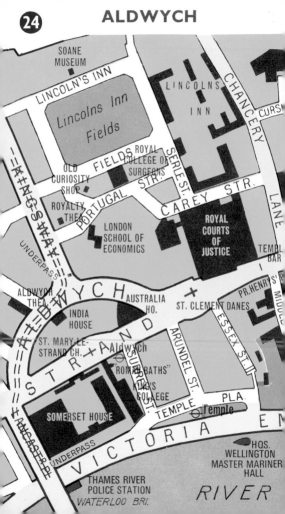

SOANE MUSEUM

LINCOLN'S INN

LINCOLNS INN

CHANCERY

Lincolns Inn Fields

CURS

LANE

OLD CURIOSITY SHOP

FIELDS

ROYAL COLLEGE OF SURGEONS

SERLE ST.

CAREY STR.

ROYALTY THEA.

PORTUGAL STR.

ROYAL COURTS OF JUSTICE

TEMPL BAR

LONDON SCHOOL OF ECONOMICS

K I N G S W A Y

UNDERPASS

A L D W Y C H

PR. HENRY'S

MIDDL

ALDWYCH THEA.

AUSTRALIA HO.

ST. CLEMENT DANES

INDIA HOUSE

ESSEX ST.

ST. MARY LE-STRAND CH.

Aldwych

S T R A N D

ARUNDEL ST.

"ROMAN" BATHS

KING'S COLLEGE

TEMPLE PLA.

SOMERSET HOUSE

Temple

UNDERPASS

V I C T O R I A

EM

HQS. WELLINGTON MASTER MARINER HALL

THAMES RIVER POLICE STATION

RIVER

WATERLOO BRI.

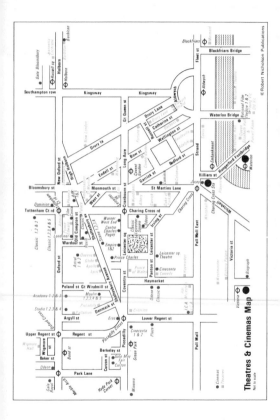

Theatres & Cinemas Map

Not to scale

© Robert Nicholson Publications

London 3

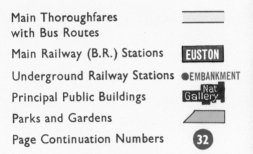

Main Thoroughfares
with Bus Routes

Main Railway (B.R.) Stations   **EUSTON**

Underground Railway Stations   ●**EMBANKMENT**

Principal Public Buildings   **Nat Gallery**

Parks and Gardens

Page Continuation Numbers   **32**

OXFORD STREET

Oxford Street, where specially marked, is closed
to through traffic (except buses and taxis)
between 7a.m. and 7p.m. Monday-Saturday

KEY MAP OVERLEAF

© GEOGRAPHIA LTD.

*Based upon the Ordnance Survey Maps with the sanction
of the Controller of H.M. Stationery Office*

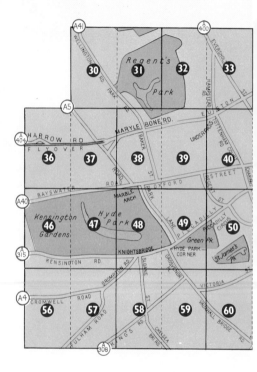

MAPS OF LONDON

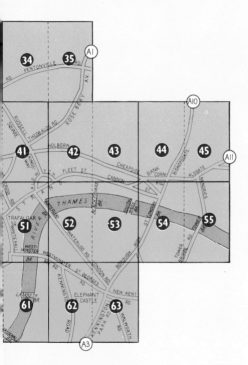

Principal Road Exits
Department of Transport Road Numbers (A2)

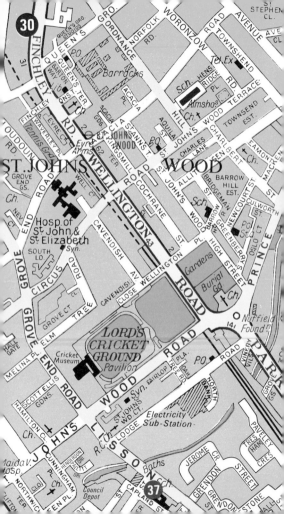

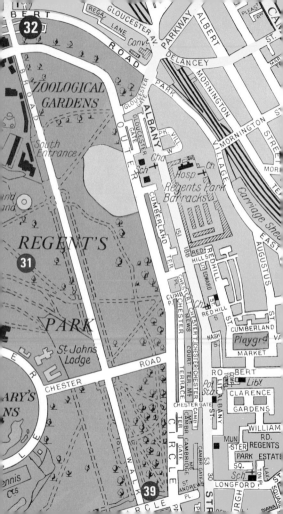

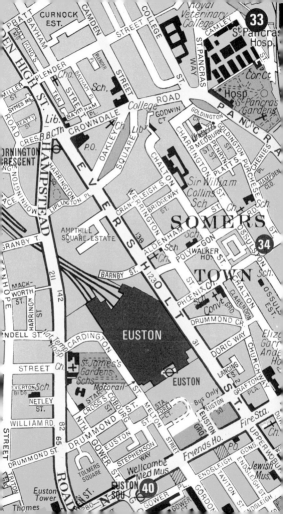

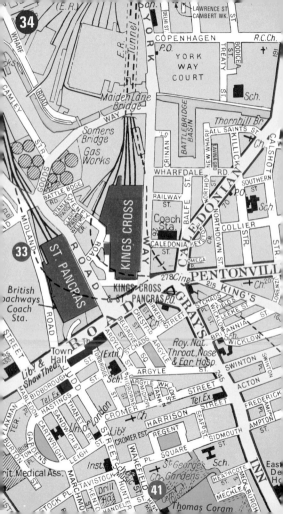

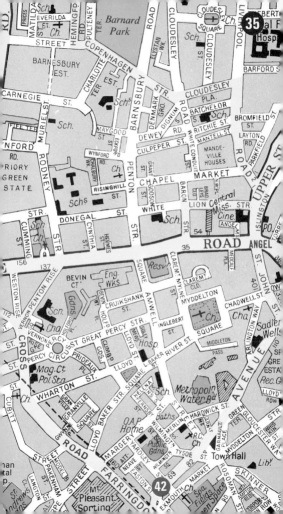

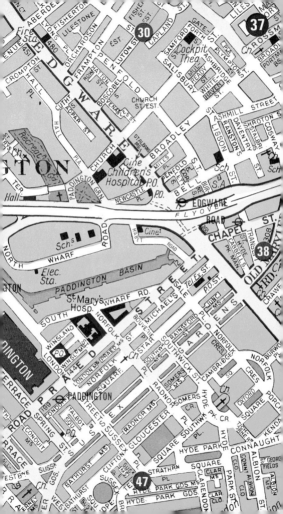

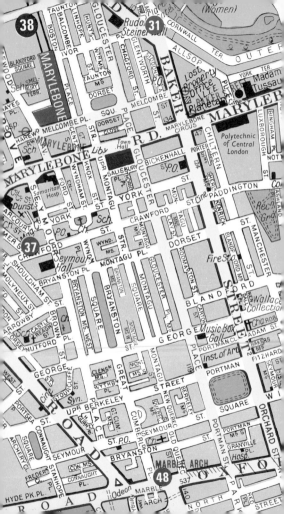

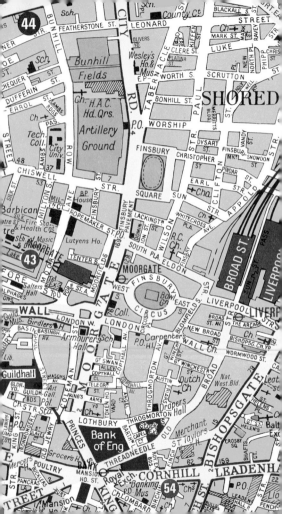

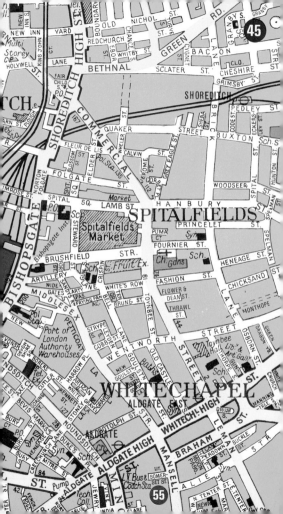

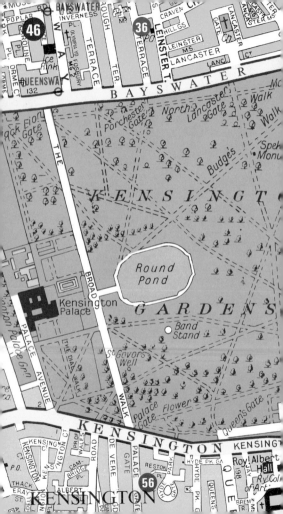

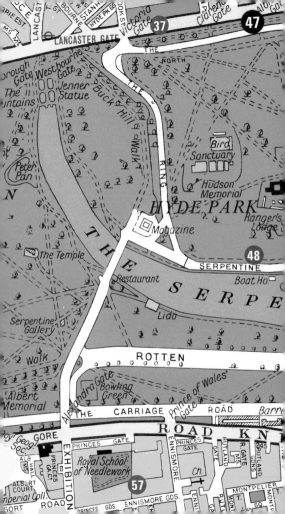

LANCASTER GATE

THE

NORTH

VICTORIA
Gate

Clarence
Gate

rough
Gate Westbourne
Gate

The
untains

Jenner
Statue

THE

BUCK Hill Walk

Peter
Pan

Bird
Sanctuary

RING

Hudson
Memorial

HYDE PARK

Ranger's
Lodge

Magazine

The Temple

SERPENTINE

Boat Ho.

THE

SERPE

Restaurant

Serpentine
Gallery

Lido

Walk

ROTTEN

Albert
Memorial

Alexandra Gate

Bowling
Green

Prince of Wales'
Gate

THE CARRIAGE ROAD Barr

GORE ROAD KN

Roy. Geog.
Soc.

ALB
HALL

PRINCES GATE

EXHIBITION

PRINCES GATE

Royal School
of Needlework

ENNISMORE

PRINCES
GATE

RUTLAND
GATE

245

RUTLAND
GDNS

R. GATE
M.S.

Ch.

IMPERIAL COLL

perial Coll

SORT ROAD

PRINCES GDS.

ENNISMORE GDS.

MONTPELIER

ENNI

RUT.

MONT

SQ.

RING

CUMBERLAND GATE

GREEN

Cumberland
Gate

Speakers
Corner

RIDE

UNRAVEN SQ
LEES

WOODS MS

UPR BROOK

ST

Underground
Car Park

CULROSS

Brook Gate

UPR GROSVE

Grosvenor
Gate

MO

Superintendents
Lodge

Fountain

Police Sta.

Res!

P A

HYDE · PARK

R

Spanhi

Boat Ho.

N T I N E

Band Stand

ROAD

HYDE PARK

ROW

UNDERPASS

THE

CARRIAGE

Albert
Gate

Minema
Sch

cks

GROSV

PARK

EDINBGH

GATE

KINNN

POY

KINNERTON

KINN

WILTON

PL

BARRACKS

WILTON ROW

G H T S B R I D G E

WILTON

Ch

SEVILLE

WILLIAM

WILTON CRES.

TREVOR

RAPHAEL ST

KNIGHTSBRIDGE

LOWNDES

WILLIAM ST

CAP
ENS
CL.

WILTON

BELGRAVE MS

TREVOR SQUARE

LANCELOT
PL

Fire
Sta.

SQUARE

PAVILN

HARRIET

NORTH

TREVOR SQ

STREET

ROAD

LO

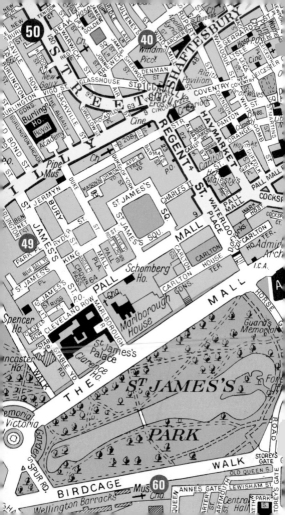

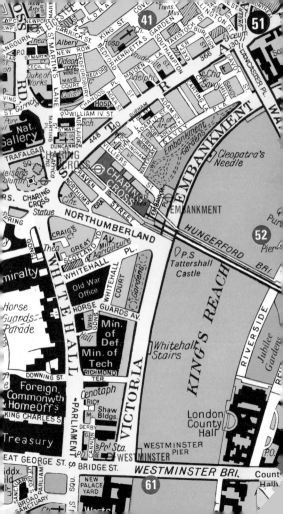

52

42

King's Coll.

TUDOR ST
TEMPLE
TALLIS ST
CARMELITE ST
JN CARPENTER S.

CROWN ST
H.W.K.
TEMPLE
Inner Temple Garden
Tel HO
Sion Coll.

FOUNTAIN
Chancery
Mid Temple

Cof Scr

TEMPLE PL

TORIA   TEMPLE   EMBANKMENT

H.M.S. President

Temple Steps

H.M.S. Chrysanthemum

UNDER

nes River
ce Sta.

H.Q.S. Wellington
Master Mariners Hall

R I V E R

K I N G S

ALY

BRI.

WATERLOO

National Film Theatre

London Weekend TV. Centre

National Theatre

BARGE HO. RD.
BODDYS BR.

GROUND

RENNIE

MILTHY WK.

UPPER   GROUND

UPPER WALL
BROAD
WALL
DUCHY ST.
COIN ST.

STREET

CHATH

PARIS GARDEN

Ch.

51
Royal Festival Hall

CONCERT HALL APP

TENISON WAY

UPPER
CORNWALL
DOON ST.
ST.
CORNWALL ST.
STAMFORD
Hosp.
P.O.

Tennis
AQUINAS ST.

PEABODY
BS Sch.

FIELD

Sch.

COLOMBO

45

Ch.

MEYMOTT ST.

WATERLOO

MEPHAM ST.

SANDELL
EXTONS ST.
WHITTLEZ SEY.
BRAD
ST.
ROUPEL

FED ST.

STREET
ROUPELL ST.

JOAN ST.

SABELLA ST.

THE CUT

WATERLOO

P.O.

Union Jack Club

WOOTTON

LIONS

ST.

GREET
WALK

Young Vic.
Theatre
Ch.

BURROWS
ST.

WATERLOO

Lib.
Old Vic

ROAD

MITRE RD
SHORTS RD.
WEBBER ST.
Rec.
RUFFORD
ROW

SOUNDAR
ST.

VALENTINE PL.
VALEN PL.

H.ST.
LEAKE ST.
Hosp.
ADDLE

MARSH ST.
STANGATE ST.

62

JOHANNA ST.
JUNCTION
Sch.

TANSWELL EST.

CORAL ST.
GRAY ST.
BARONS PL.

WEBBER ROW

Sch.

PEABODY

WESTM

LOWER
GRINDAL
TRPI
ST.

RO

43 **53**

QUEEN
Coll. of Arms
VICTORIA

Mermaid Thea.
S.A.H.Q.
Painters
Hall

PUDDLE DOCK

BLACKFRIARS

BLACKFRIARS
BRI.

Queenhithe Dock

T H A M E
Southwark Br. Steps
Southwark BR.

R E A C H

BANKSIDE

BANKS.

Power
Sta.

Skin Mkt.

Bear Gds.

Rose Al.

Mus.

ST. HOLLAND ST.

HOPTON ST.

Hopton's
Almsho.

SUMNER

PARK ST.

EMERSON PL.

EMERSON

ST.

STREET

Shakespeare
Memorial

PARK ST.

54

SOUTHWARK

142

FALCON

GREAT

ROAD

SUMNER
BGS.

SOUTHWAR

BURRELL S.

BEAR L.

95

PRICES

FARNHAM

146

THRALE S.

230

P.O.

NICHOLSON S.

TREV. ST.

Sch.

LAVINGTON ST.

42

SCORESBY S.

DOLBEN S.

GAMBIA

SUFFOLK

EWER

SOUTHWARK
GR.
WARDENS
GR.

KEPPEL RW.
AMERICA S.

59

ST.

STREET

UNION SCH.

R.c.Ch

POMEROY

UNION

UNION
ST.

RISBOROUGH ST.

Sch.

Duthy
Hall

PEPPER ST.

BRIDGE

AYRES ST.

GdNs.

QUILP ST.

REDCROSS ST.

RED-
CROSS

STANHOPE S.

ST.

DORRIT ST.

NELSON
SQU.

COPPERFIELD

SARGENT

LOMAN

SAWYER

ST.

HOSIER

MARSHALSEA RD.

QUILP ST.

BOROUGH

SURREY ROW

POCOCK

KING'S BENCH

GLASSHILL

GREAT

POCOCK ST.

Playga

Fire
Sta.

HOSB

STURGE

LANT ST.

TOULMIN ST.

SOUTHWARK

ST.

PICKWICK

ST.

STREET

BOROUGH

CKFRIARS

Sch.
S.A.

RUSHWORTH

WEBBER

LANCAS.

KING'S BENCH

HILL ST.

SUFFOLK

BELVEDERE

BITTERN

ST.

63

STREET

230

P.O.

ROAD

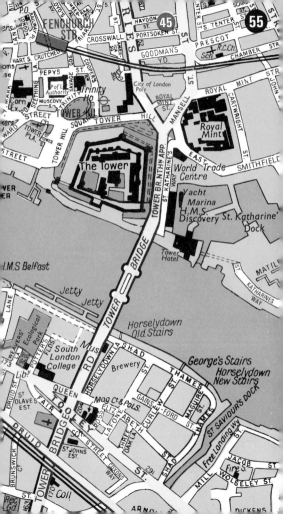

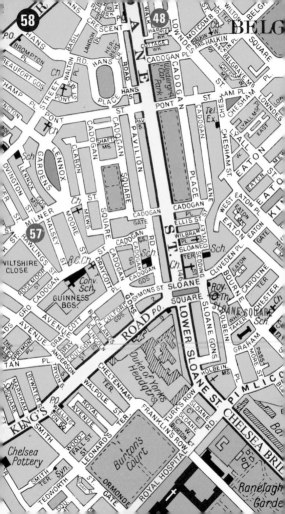

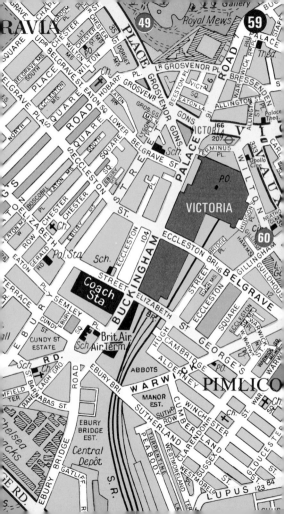

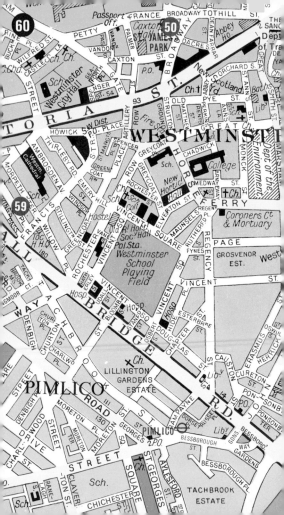

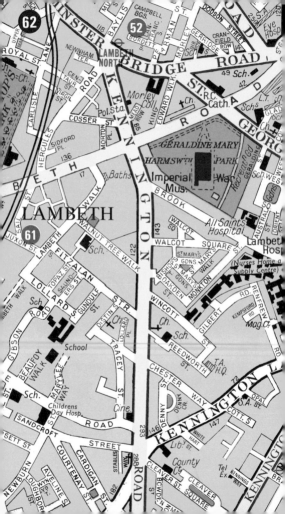

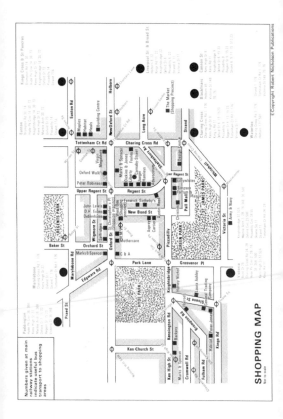

SHOPPING MAP

Not to scale

© Copyright Robert Nicholson Publications

Index 4

ABBREVIATIONS

Arc. — Arcade
Av. — Avenue
Bri. — Bridge
Bldgs. — Buildings
Cir. — Circus
Clo. — Close
Cotts. — Cottages
Ct. — Court
Cres. — Crescent
Dr. — Drive
E. — East
Embk. — Embankment
Est. — Estate

Gdns. — Gardens
Gte. — Gate
Gt. — Great
Gn. — Green
Gro. — Grove
Hl. — Hill
Ho. — House
La. — Lane
Lit. — Little
Lwr. — Lower
Mans. — Mansion
Mkt. — Market
Ms. — Mews

N. — North
Pass. — Passage
Pl. — Place
Rd. — Road
S. — South
Sq. — Square
St. — Street
Ter. — Terrace
Upr. — Upper
Vill. — Villas
Wk. — Walk
W. — West
Yd. — Yard

Note: (1) The letters A or B precede the map page number and indicate whether the street is to be found in the upper half of the page (A), or (B) on the lower half.

(2) Certain streets named in the index are to be found in both the Central London and London map sections. In order to distinguish between the two, the name of the street that is duplicated is given first in a bold type for the Central London section, followed immediately by the same name in ordinary type for the London section.

Abbey Orchard St. SW1	A60	
Abbots La. SE1	B54	
Abbots Manor SE1 SW1	B59	
Abchurch La. EC4	A54	
Aberdeen Pl. NW8	B30	
Abingdon St. SW1	A61	
Acacia Gdns. NW8	A30	
Acacia Pl. NW8	A30	
Acacia Rd. NW8	A30	
Achilles Way W1	B49	
Acton St. WC1	B34	
Adam & Eve Ct. W1	B40	
Adam's Row W1	A49	
Adam St.	**21**	
Adam St. W1	B38	
Adam St. WC2	A51	
Addington St. SE1	B52	
Addle Hl. EC4	B43	
Adelaide St.	**23**	
Adelaide St. WC2	A51	
Adeline Pl. WC1	B40	
Adelphi Ter. WC2	A51	
Adpar St. W2	A37	
Agar St.	**21**	
Agar St. WC2	A51	
Air St. W1	B50	
Albany St. NW1	B32	
Albany Ter. NW1	B32	
Albany, The W1	A50	
Albemarle St.	**19**	
Albemarle St. W1	A49	
Alberta Est. SE17	B63	
Alberta St. SE17	B63	
Albert Embk. SE1	B61	
Albert Hall Ms. SW7	A57	
Albert Ms. W8	A57	
Albert Pl. W8	A57	
Albert St. NW1	A32	
Albert Ter. NW1	A31	
Albion Ms. W2	B37	
Albion Pl. EC1	A43	
Albion St. W2	B37	
Aldenham St. NW1	A33	
Aldermanbury EC2	B43	
Aldermanbury Sq. EC2	B43	
Alderney St. W1	B59	
Alders Gte. EC1	A43	
Aldford St. W1	A49	
Aldgate EC3	B44	
Aldgate High St. EC3	B45	
Aldwych	**24**	
Aldwych WC2	B42	
Alexander Pl. SW7	A57	
Alexander Sq. SW3	A57	
Alfred Ms. W1	A40	
Alfred Pl. WC1	A40	
Alie St. E1	B45	
Allhallows La. EC4	B44	
Allington St. SW1	A59	
Allitsen Rd. NW8	A30	
All Saints St. N1	A34	
Allsop Pl. NW1	A38	
All Souls Pl. W1	B39	
Alpha Clo. NW1	A37	
Ambergate St. SE17	B63	
Ambrosden Av. SW1	A60	
Amelia St. SE17	B63	
Amen Ct. EC4	B43	
America Sq. EC3	A55	
America St. SE1	B53	
Ampthill Sq. Est. NW1	A33	
Ampton Pl. WC1	B34	
Ampton St. WC1	B34	
Amwell St. EC1	B35	
Anderson St. SW8	B58	
Angel Ct. EC2	B44	
Angel Ct. SW1	B50	
Angel Ms. N1	A35	
Angel Pl. EC4	B54	
Angel Pl. SE1	A54	
Angel St. EC1	B43	
Ann's Clo. SW1	B48	
Ansdell St. W8	A46	
Ansdell Ter. W8	A46	
Appletree Yd. SW1	A50	
Appold St. EC2	A44	
Aquila St. NW8	A30	
Aquinas St. SE1	B52	
Arcade, The EC2	B44	
Archer St. W1	A50	
Archery Clo. W2	B38	
Arch St. SE1	A63	
Argent St. SE1	B53	
Argyle St. WC1	B34	
Argyle Wk. WC1	B34	
Argyll St. W1	B40	
Arlington Rd. NW1	A33	
Arlington Sq. N1	A50	
Arlington St. SW1	A50	
Arlington Way EC1	B35	
Arne St. WC2	B41	
Arneway St. SW1	A61	
Arthur Ct. W2	B36	
Arthur St. EC4	A54	
Artillery La. E1	B44	
Artillery Pass. E1	B45	
Artillery Row SW1	A59	
Artizan St. E1	B45	
Arundel St.	**24**	
Arundel St. WC2	A52	
Ashbridge St. NW8	A38	
Ashburn Gdns. SW7	A56	
Ashburn Ms. SW7	A56	
Ashburn Pl. SW7	A56	
Ashland Pl. W1	A38	
Ashmill St. NW1	A37	
Ash Pl. SW1	A59	
Assam St. E1	B45	
Astell St. SW3	B57	
Aster Pl. SE1	B58	
Astwood Ms. SW7	A56	
Atherstone Ms. SW7	B58	
Atterbury St. SW1	B61	
Attneave St. WC1	B35	
Auden Pl. NW1	A30	
Audley St. W1	A58	
Augustus St. NW1	B32	
Austin Friars EC2	B44	
Austral St. SE11	B62	
Aveline St. SE11	B62	
Ave Maria La. EC4	A54	
Avenue Clo. NW8	A31	
Avenue Rd. NW8	A31	
Avenue, The EC3	A54	
Avery Row	**18**	
Avery Row W1	A49	
Avonmouth St. SE1	A63	
Avon Pl. SE1	A63	
Aybrook St. W1	A39	
Aylesbury Rd. SE17	B63	
Aylesbury St. EC1	A43	
Aylesford St. SW1	B60	
Ayres St. SE1	B53	
Babmaes St. SW1	A50	
Back Gravel La. E1	B45	
Back Hl. EC1	A42	
Baden Pl. SE1	A54	
Bainbridge St. WC1	B41	
Bakers Ms. W1	B38	
Baker's Row EC1	A52	

Street	Ref		Street	Ref		Street	Ref
Baker St. NW1	A38		Beak St. W1	A50		Berners Pl. W1	B40
Balcombe St. NW1	A38		Bear Alley EC4	B43		Berners Rd. N1	A35
Balderton St. W1	A38		Bear Gdns. SE1	A53		Berners St. W1	B40
Baldwin's Gdns. EC1	A42		Bear La. SE1	B53		Berryfield Rd. SE17	B63
Balfe St. N1	A34		Bear St. WC2	A50		Berry St. EC1	A43
Balfour Ms. W1	A48		Beatty St. NW1	A33		**Berwick St.**	**19**
Baltic St. EC1	A43		Beauchamp Pl. SW3	A57		Berwick St. W1	B40
Bankend SE1	B53		Beauchamp St. EC1	A42		Bessborough Gdns. SW1	B60
Bankside SE1	A52		Beaufort Gdns. SW3	A58		Bessborough Pl. SW1	B60
Bankside SE1	B53		Beaufoy Wk. SE11	B62		Bessborough St. SW1	B60
Banner St. EC1	A43		Beaumont Ms. W1	A39		Bessborough Way SW1	B60
Barge House Rd. SE1			Beaumont Pl. W1	A40		Bethnal Gn. Rd. E1	A45
Bark Pl. W1	A46		Beaumont St. W1	A39		Betterton St. WC2	B41
Barlow Pl. W1	A49		Bedale St. SE1	B54		Bevin Ct. WC1	B35
Barnby St. NW1	B33		Bedford Av. WC1	B40		Bevin Way WC1	B35
Barnesbury Est. N1	A35		Bedfordbury WC2	A51		Bevis Marks EC3	B45
Barnham St. SE1	B54		Bedford Ct. WC2	A51		Bickenhall St. W1	A38
Barnsbury Rd. N1	A35		Bedford Pl. WC1	A41		Bidborough St. WC1	B34
Baron's Pl. SE1	B52		Bedford Row WC1	A42		Billiter St. EC3	A55
Baron St. N1	A35		Bedford Sq. WC1	A40		Bina Gdns. SW5	B56
Barrett St. W1	B39		**Bedford St.**	**21**		Bingham Pl. W1	A38
Barrie Est. W2	A47		Bedford St. WC2	A51		Binney St. W1	B39
Barron Clo. WC1	A41		Bedford Way WC1	A41		Birchin La. EC3	B44
Barrow Hl. Est. NW8	A30		Beech St. EC2	A43		Birdcage Wk. SW1	B50
Barrow Hl. NW8	A30		Beeston Pl. SW1	A59		Bird St. W1	B39
Barter St. WC1	B41		Belgrave Ms. N. SW1	A58		Birkenhead St. WC1	B34
Bartholomew Clo. EC1	B43		Belgrave Ms. S. SW1	A59		Bishops Bri. Rd. W2	B36
Bartholomew La. EC2	B44		Belgrave Ms. W. SW1	A58		Bishops Ct. EC4	B43
Bartlett Ct. EC4	B42		Belgrave Pl. SW1	A59		Bishops Ct. WC2	B42
Bartletts Pass. EC4	B42		Belgrave Rd. SW1	B59		Bishopsgate Ch. Yd. EC2	B44
Barton St. SW1	A61		Belgrave Sq. SW1	A58		Bishopsgate EC2	
Barton Way NW8	A30		Belgrove St. WC1	B34		Bishop's Ter. SE11	B62
Basil St. SW3	A58		Bell La. E1	B45		Bittern St. SE1	B53
Basinghall Av. EC2	B43		Bell St. NW1	A37		Blackburne's Ms. W1	A48
Basinghall St. EC2	B43		Bell Yd. WC2	B42		**Blackfriars Bri.**	**25**
Bastwick St. EC1	A43		Belvedere Bldgs. SE1	B53		**Blackfriars La.**	**25**
Batchelor St. N1	A35		Belvedere Pl. SE1	A63		Blackfriars La. EC4	A53
Bateman St. W1	B40		Belvedere Rd. SE1	B51		Blackfriars Pass. EC4	A53
Bath Ter. SE1	A63		Bemerton St. N1	A34		Blackfriars Rd. SE1	A62
Bathurst Ms. W2	B37		Bendall Ms. NW1	A38		Blacklands Ter. SW3	B58
Bathurst St. W2	B37		Benjamin St. EC1	A43		Black Prince Rd. SE1	B61
Battle Bri. La. SE1	B54		Bennet St. SW1	A50		Blandford Ms. W1	A38
Battle Bri. Rd. NW1	A34		Bentinck Ms. W1	B39		Blandford Sq. NW1	A38
Batt Ms. NW1	A33		Bentinck St. W1	B39		Blandford St. W1	B39
Batt St. NW1	A33		Berkeley Ms. W1	B38		Blenheim St. W1	B39
Bayham Pl. NW1	A33		**Berkeley Sq.**	**18**		Blomfield Rd. W9	A36
Bayham St. NW1	A33		Berkeley Sq. W1	A49		Blomfield St. EC2	B44
Bayley St. WC1	B40		**Berkeley St.**	**18**		Blomfield Vill. W2	A36
Baylis Rd. SE1	A62		Bermondsey St. SE1	B54			
Bayswater Rd. W2	A46		Bernard St. WC1	A41			
Beak St.	**19**		Berners Ms. W1	B40			

Name	Ref	Name	Ref	Name	Ref
Bloomburg St. SW1	B60	Brad St. SE1	B52	Broadwick St. W1	B40
Bloomfield Ter. SW1	B58	Braganza St. SE17	B62	Broad Yd. EC1	A42
Bloomsbury Pl. WC1	A41	Braham St. E1	B45	Brockam St. SE1	A63
Bloomsbury Sq. WC1	A41	Braidwood St. SE1	B54	Bromfield St. N1	A35
Bloomsbury St. WC1	B41	Bramham Gdns. SW5	B56	Brompton Pl. SW3	A58
Bloomsbury Way WC1	B41	Brandon St. SE17	A63	Brompton Rd. SW3	B56
Blossom St. E1	A45	Brandon St. SE17	B63	Brompton Sq. SW3	A57
Blue Ball Yd. SW1	B50	Brangton Rd. SE11	B62	Brook Dr. SE11	A62
Boadicea St. N1	A34	Bray Pl. SW3	B57	Brooke's Ct. EC1	A42
Boddy's Bri. SE1	A52	Bread St. EC4	B43	Brooke St. EC1	A42
Bolsover St. W1	A39	Breams Bldgs. EC4	B42	Brook Ms. W2	B36
Bolt Ct. EC4	B42	Brechin Pl. SW7	B56	Brook's Ms. W1	A49
Bolton Gdns. Ms. SW10	B56	Bremen Rd. SW7	B46	**Brook St.**	**18**
Bolton Gdns. SW5	B56	Brendon St. W1	B37	Brook St. W1	A49
Boltons, The SW10	B56	Bressenden Pl. SW1	A59	Brook St. W2	B37
Bolton St. W1	A50	**Brewer St.**	**19**	Brown Hart Gdns. W1	B38
Bonhill St. EC2	A44	Brewer St. W1	A50	Browning Est. SE17	A63
Booths Pl. W1	B40	Brew House Yd. EC1	A43	Browning Ms. W1	A39
Borers St. E1	B45	Brick St. W1	B49	Browning St. SE17	A63
Borough High St. SE1	A63	**Bride La.**	**25**	Brownlow Ms. WC1	A42
Borough Rd. SE1	A63	Bridewell Pl. EC4	B42	Brownlow St. WC1	A42
Boscobel Pl. SW1	A59	Bridford Ms. W1	A39	Broxwood Way NW8	A31
Boscobel St. NW8	A37	Bridgeman St. NW8	A30	Brune St. E1	B45
Boss St. SE1	B55	Bridge Pl. SW1	B59	Brunswick Ct. SE1	B55
Boston Pl. NW1	A38	Bridge St. SW1	B51	Brunswick Sq. WC1	A41
Boswell Ct. WC1	A41	Bridgewater Highwalk EC1	A43	Brushfield St. E1	B45
Boswell St. WC1	A41	Bridgewater Sq. EC2	A43	Bruton La. W1	A49
Botolph La. EC3	B44	Bridgewater St. EC2	A43	**Bruton Pl.**	**18**
Boundary Row SE1	B52	Bridgeway St. NW1	A33	Bruton Pl. W1	A49
Bourchier St. W1	B40	Bridle La. W1	A50	**Bruton St.**	**18**
Bourdon Pl. W1	A49	Briset St. EC1	A43	Bruton St. W1	A49
Bourdon St. W1	A49	Bristol Gdns. W9	A36	Bryanston Ms. E. W1	B38
Bourlet Clo. W1	B40	Bristol Ms. W9	A36	Bryanston Ms. W. W1	B38
Bourne St. EC1	A42	Britannia St. WC1	B34	Bryanston Pl. W1	B38
Bourne St. SW1	B58	Britten St. SW3	B57	Bryanston Sq. W1	B38
Bourne Ter. W2	A36	Britton St. EC1	A43	Bryanston St. W1	B38
Bouverie Pl. W2	B37	Broadbent St. W1	A49	Buckingham Gte. SW1	B59
Bouverie St.	**25**	Broad Ct. WC2	B41	Buckingham Palace Rd. SW	B59
Bouverie St. EC4	B42	Broadley Portman Bldgs. NW1	A31	Buckingham Pl. SW1	B59
Bowden St. SE11	B62	Broadley St. NW8	A37	Buckingham St. WC2	B59
Bow La. EC4	A54	Broad Sanctuary SW1	B51	Bucklersbury EC4	B44
Bowling Gn. La. EC1	A42	Broad St. Av. EC2	B44	Buckler St. EC4	B44
Bowling Gn. Pl. SE1	B54	Broad St. W1	A49	Buckle St. E1	B45
Bow St.	**21**	Broad Wk. NW1	A32	Bucknall St. WC2	B41
Bow St. WC2	B41	Broad Wk., The W8	A46	Budge Row EC4	A54
Boyfield St. SE1	B53	Broad Wk. W1	A48	Bulinga St. SW1	B61
Boyle St. W1	A49	Broadwall SE1	A52	Bulls Gdns. SW3	A57
Brackley St. EC1	A43	Broadway SW1	A60	Bulls Head Pl. EC3	B44
Braden St. W9	A36	**Broadwick St.**	**19**	Bull Wharf La. EC4	A53
Bradleys Clo. N1	A35			Bulst Pl. W1	B39

Bulstrode St. W1	B39	
Bunhill Row EC1	A44	
Burdett St. SE1	A62	
Burleigh St. WC2	A51	
Burlington Arc. W1	A50	
Burlington Gdns.	**19**	
Burlington Gdns. W1	A50	
Burman St. SE1	A63	
Burne St. NW1	A37	
Burnsall St. SW3	B57	
Burrell St. SE1	B53	
Burrows Ms. SE1	B52	
Burton Pl. WC1	B34	
Burton St. WC1	B34	
Burwood Pl. W2	B37	
Bury Ct. EC3	B45	
Bury St. EC3	B45	
Bury St. SW1	A50	
Bury Wk. SW3	B57	
Bush La. EC4	A54	
Bute St. SW7	A57	
Buxton St. E1	A45	
Byng Pl. WC1	A40	
Byward St. EC3	B44	
Bywater St. SW3	B58	
Cabell St. NW1	A37	
Cadogan Gdns. SW1	A58	
Cadogan Gte. SW1	A58	
Cadogan La. SW1	A58	
Cadogan Pl. SW1	A58	
Cadogan Sq. SW1	A58	
Cadogan St. SW3	B58	
Caleb St. SE1	B53	
Caledonian Rd. N1	B44	
Caledonia St. N1	A34	
Cale St. SW3	B57	
Calshot St. N1	A34	
Calthorpe St. WC1	A42	
Calvin St. E1	A45	
Cambert Wk. NW1	A34	
Cambridge Circus	**20**	
Cambridge Cir. WC2	B40	
Cambridge Gte. Ms. NW1	B32	
Cambridge Gte. NW1	B32	
Cambridge Pl. W8	B46	
Cambridge Sq. W2	A37	
Cambridge St. SW1	B59	
Cambridge Ter. Ms. NW1	B32	
Cambridge Ter. NW1	B32	
Camden High St. NW1	A32	
Camden St. NW1	A33	
Camlet St. E2	A45	
Camley St. NW1	A33	
Camomile St. EC3	B44	
Campbell Bldgs. SE1	A62	
Camperdown St. E1	B45	
Candover St. W1	A40	
Canning Pass. W8	A56	
Canning Pass. W8	B46	
Canning Pl. W8	A56	
Cannon Row SW1	B51	
Cannon St. EC4	B43	
Canterbury Pl. SE17	B63	
Capel Ct. EC2	B44	
Capland St. NW8	A37	
Capper St. WC1	A40	
Carburton St. W1	A39	
Cardigan Gdns. SW1	F9	
Cardigan St. SE11	B62	
Cardington St. NW1	B33	
Carey La. EC2	B43	
Carey St.	**24**	
Carey St. WC2	B42	
Carlisle Av. EC3	A55	
Carlisle La. SE1	A62	
Carlisle Pl. SW1	A59	
Carlisle St. W1	B40	
Carlos Pl.	**18**	
Carlos Pl. W1	A49	
Carlton Gdns.	**22**	
Carlton Gdns. SW1	B50	
Carlton House Ter.	**22**	
Carlton Ho. Ter. SW1	B50	
Carlton St. SW1	A50	
Carlyle Sq. SW3	B57	
Carmelite St. EC4	A52	
Carnaby St.	**19**	
Carnaby St. W1	B40	
Carnegie St. N1	A35	
Caroline Pl. W2	A46	
Caroline Ter. SW1	B58	
Carpenters Clo. SW1	B48	
Carpenter St. W1	A49	
Carrington St. W1	A49	
Carter La. EC4	B43	
Carter St. SW1	B50	
Carthusian St. EC1	A43	
Carting La.	**21**	
Carting La. WC2	A51	
Carton St. W1	B38	
Cartwright Gdns. WC1	B34	
Cartwright St. E1	A55	
Casson St. E1	B45	
Castellain Rd. W9	A36	
Castle La. SW1	A60	
Castlereagh St. W1	B38	
Castle St. EC1	A42	
Cathedral Pl. EC4	B43	
Cathedral St. SE1	B54	
Catherine Pl. SW1	A60	
Catherine St.	**21**	
Catherine St. WC2	A51	
Cato St. W1	B38	
Catton St. WC1	B41	
Causton St. SW1	B60	
Cavaye Pl. SW10	B56	
Cavendish Av. NW8	A30	
Cavendish Clo. NW8	B30	
Cavendish Pl. W1	B39	
Cavendish Sq.	**18**	
Cavendish Sq. W1	B39	
Caxton St. SW1	A60	
Cecil Ct. WC2	A51	
Celbridge Ms. W2	B36	
Centaur St. SE1	A62	
Central Mkts. EC1	B43	
Cerney Ms. W2	B37	
Chadwell St. EC1	B35	
Chadwick St. SW1	A60	
Chagford St. NW1	A38	
Chalbury Wk. N1	A35	
Chalton St. NW1	A33	
Chambers St. SE16	B55	
Chamber St. E1	A55	
Chancel St. SE1	B53	
Chancery La.	**24**	
Chancery La. WC2	B42	
Chance St. E2	A45	
Chandos Pl.	**21**	
Chandos Pl. WC2	A51	
Chandos St. W1	B39	
Chapel Mkt. N1	A35	
Chapel Pl. W1	B39	
Chapel St. NW1	A37	
Chapel St. SW1	A59	
Chapter St. SW1	B60	
Charing Cross Rd.	**20**	
Charing Cross Rd. WC2	B40	
Charing Cross	**22**	
Charing Cross WC2	A51	
Charlbert St. NW8	A30	

Charles II St.	**22**	
Charles II St. SW1	A50	
Charles La. NW8	A30	
Charles St. W1	A49	
Charleston St. SE17	B63	
Charlotte Pl. W1	B40	
Charlotte Rd. EC2	A44	
Charlotte Ter. N1	A35	
Charlwood Pl. SW1	B60	
Charlwood St. SW1	B60	
Charrington St. NW1	A33	
Charterhouse Bldgs. EC1	A43	
Charterhouse Ms. EC1	A43	
Charterhouse Sq. EC1	A43	
Charterhouse St. EC1	A43	
Charterhouse St. EC1	A43	
Charterhouse St. EC1	B42	
Cheapside EC2	B43	
Chelsea Bri. Rd. SW1	A58	
Chelsea Cloisters SW3	B57	
Chelsea Manor Gdns. SW3	B57	
Chelsea Manor St. SW3	B57	
Chelsea Sq. SW3	B57	
Cheltenham Ter. SW3	B58	
Cheney Rd. NW1	A34	
Chenies Pl. NW1	A33	
Chenies St. WC1	A40	
Chequer St. EC1	A44	
Chesham Ms. SW1	A58	
Chesham Pl. SW1	A58	
Chesham St. SW1	A58	
Cheshire Clo. E2	A45	
Cheshire St. E2	A45	
Chester Clo. SW1	B49	
Chester Ct. NW1	B32	
Chesterfield Gdns. W1	A49	
Chesterfield Hl. W1	A49	
Chesterfield St. W1	A49	
Chester Gte. NW1	B32	
Chester Ms. SW1	A39	
Chester Pl. NW1	B32	
Chester Rd. NW1	B32	
Chester Row SW1	B58	
Chester Sq. SW1	A59	
Chester St. SW1	A59	
Chester Ter. Ms. NW1	B32	
Chester Ter. NW1	B32	
Chester Way SE11	B62	
Cheval Pl. SW7	A57	
Chicheley St. SE1	B51	
Chichester Rents WC2	B42	
Chichester St. SW1	B60	
Chichester St. W2	A36	
Chicksand Est. E1	A45	
Chicksand St. E1	B45	
Chiltern St. W1	A38	
Chilton St. E2	A45	
Chilworth Ms. W2	B36	
Chilworth St. W2	B36	
Chiswell St. EC1	A44	
Chitty St. W1	A40	
Christina St. EC2	A44	
Christopher St. EC2	A44	
Church Est. NW8	A37	
Church St. W2	A37	
Churchway NW1	B33	
Church Yd. Row SE11	B63	
Churton Pl. SW1	B60	
Churton St. SW1	B60	
Circular Rd. SE1	A63	
Circus Pl. EC2	A44	
Circus Rd. NW8	B30	
City Rd. EC1	B35	
City Rd. EC1	A44	
Clabon Ms. SW1	A58	
Clare Mkt. WC2	B41	
Claremont Clo. N1	B35	
Claremont Sq. N1	B35	
Clarence Gdns. NW1	B32	
Clarence Pass. NW1	A34	
Clarence Ter. NW1	A38	
Clarence Yd. SE17	B63	
Clarendon Clo. W2	B37	
Clarendon Gdns. W9	A36	
Clarendon Gro. NW1	B33	
Clarendon Ms. W2	B37	
Clarendon Pl. W2	B37	
Clarendon St. SW1	B59	
Clarendon Ter. W9	A36	
Clareville Gro. SW7	B56	
Clareville St. SW7	B56	
Clarges Ms. W1	A49	
Clarges St. W1	A49	
Claverton St. SW1	B60	
Clay St. W1	A38	
Cleaver Sq. SE11	B62	
Cleaver St. SE11	B62	
Cleeve Yd. SW1	A50	
Clements Inn Pass. WC2	B42	
Clements Inn WC2	B42	
Clements La. EC4	B42	
Clennam St. SE1	B53	
Clenston Ms. W1	B38	
Clere Pl. EC2	A44	
Clere St. EC2	A44	
Clerkenwell Clo. EC1	A42	
Clerkenwell Gn. EC1	A42	
Clerkenwell Rd. EC1	A42	
Cleveland Gdns. W2	B36	
Cleveland Ms. W1	A40	
Cleveland Row SW1	B50	
Cleveland Sq. W2	B36	
Cleveland St. W1	A39	
Cleveland Ter. W2	B36	
Clifford St.	**19**	
Clifford St. W1	A49	
Clifton Ct. NW8	B30	
Clifton Gdns. W9	A36	
Clifton Rd. W9	A36	
Clifton St. EC2	A44	
Clifton Ter. W2	B37	
Clifton Vill. W9	A36	
Clink St. SE1	A54	
Clipstone Ms. W1	A40	
Clipstone St. W1	A39	
Cliveden Pl. SW1	B58	
Cloak La. EC4	A54	
Clock Pl. SE1	B63	
Cloth Fair EC1	B43	
Cloudesley Pl. N1	A35	
Cloudesley Rd. N1	A35	
Cloudesley Sq. N1	A35	
Cloudesley St. N1	A35	
Club Row E2	A45	
Coach & Horses Yd. W1	A49	
Cobb St. E1	B45	
Coburg St. NW1	B33	
Cochrane St. NW8	A30	
Cock La. EC1	B43	
Cockpit Yd. WC1	A42	
Cockspur Ct. SW1	A50	
Cockspur St.	**22**	
Cockspur St. SW1	A50	
Code St. E1	A45	
Coin St. SE1	A52	
Colbeck Ms. SW7	B56	
Coldbath St. EC1	A42	
Coleherne Ct. SW5	B56	
Coleman St. EC2	B44	

Cole St. SE1	A63	Cornwall Gdns. Wk.	A56	Crawford St. W1	B38
Coley St. WC1	A42	SW7		Crawford St. W1	A38
College Gro. NW1	A33	Cornwall Ms. S. SW7	A56	Crecent, The EC3	A55
College Hl. EC4	A54	Cornwall Rd. SE1	A52	Creechurch La. EC3	B45
College Pl. NW1	A33	Cornwall Ter. NW1	A38	Creed La. EC4	B43
College St. EC4	A54	Corporation Row EC1	A42	Cresswell Gdns. SW5	B56
College St. NW1	A33	Cosmo Pl. WC1	A41	Cresswell Pl. SW10	B56
Collier St. N1	A34	Cosser St. SE1	A62	Crestfield St. WC1	B34
Collingham Gdns.	B56	Cosway St. NW1	A37	Crinan St. N1	A34
SW5		Cotham St. SE17	B63	Cripplegate St. EC1	A43
Collingham Pl. SW5	A56	Cottage Pl. SW3	A57	Crispin St. E1	B45
Collingham Rd. SW5	A56	Cottage Wk. SW1	A58	Cromer Est. WC1	B34
Colnbrook St. SE1	A62	Cottesmore Gdns. W8	A56	Cromer St. WC1	B34
Colombo St. SE1	B52	Cottington St. SE11	B62	Crompton St. W2	A37
Colonnade WC1	A41	Coulson St. SW3	B58	Cromwell Ms. SW7	B57
Colville Pl. W1	A40	Courtenay St. SE11	B62	Cromwell Pl. SW7	A57
Colworth Gro. SE17	B63	Courtfield Gdns. SW5	B56	Crosby Row SE1	B54
Commercial Rd. E1	B45	Courtfield Ms. SW7	B56	Crosby Sq. EC3	B44
Commercial St. E1	A45	Courtfield Rd. SW7	B56	Cross Keys Clo. W1	B39
Compton Clo. NW1	B32	Cousin La. EC4	A54	Crosswall EC3	A55
Compton Pass. EC1	A43	Covent Garden	21	Crown Ct. WC2	B41
Compton St. EC1	A43	Covent Gdn. WC2	A51	Crowndale Rd. NW1	A33
Concert Hall App. SE1	B52	Coventry St.	20	Crown Office Row EC4	A52
Conduit Ms. W2	B37	Coventry St. W1	A50	Crown Pass. SW1	B50
Conduit Pl. W2	B37	Cowcross St. EC1	A42	Crucifix La. SE1	B54
Conduit St.	**18**	Cowley St. SW1	A61	Cruikshank St. WC1	B35
Conduit St. W1	A49	Cowper St. EC2	A44	Crutched Friars EC3	A55
Connaught Clo. W2	B37	Coxons Way SE1	B55	Cubitt St. WC1	B35
Connaught Pl. W2	B38	Cox's Ct. EC1	B43	Culford Gdns. SW1	B58
Connaught Sq. W2	B38	Coxson Pl. SE1	B55	Cullum St. EC3	A54
Connaught St. W2	B37	Craig's Ct. SW1	A51	Culpepper St. N1	A34
Cons St. SE1	B52	Cramer St. W1	A39	Culross St. W1	A48
Constitution Hl. SW1	B49	Crampton St. SE17	B63	Culworth St. NW8	A30
Content St. SE17	B63	**Cranbourn St.**	**20**	Cumberland Gdns.	B35
Conway Ms. W1	A39	Cranbourn St. WC2	A50	WC1	
Cooper's La. WC1	A34	Cranfield Row SE1	A62	Cumberland Gte. W1	B38
Cooper's Row EC3	A55	Cranleigh St. NW1	A33	Cumberland Mkt. NW1	B32
Copenhagen St. N1	A34	Cranley Gdns. SW7	B56	Cumberland Pl. NW1	B32
Copenhagen St. N1	A35	Cranley Ms. SW7	B56	Cumberland St. SW1	B59
Copperfield St. SE1	B53	Cranley Pl. SW7	B57	Cumberland Ter. NW1	A32
Copthall Av. EC2	B44	Cranmer Ct. SW3	B57	Cumming St. N1	A35
Copthall Clo. EC2	B44	Craven Hl. Gdns. W2	B36	Cundy St. Est. SW1	B59
Coptic St. WC1	B41	Craven Hl. W2	B36	Cundy St. SW1	B59
Coral St. SE1	B52	Craven Hl. Ms. W2	B36	Cunningham Pl. NW8	B30
Coram St. WC1	A41	Craven Pl. WC2	A51	Cureton St. SW1	B60
Corbet Pl. E1	A45	Craven Rd. W2	B36	Curlew St. SE1	B55
Cork St.	**19**	**Craven St.**	**23**	Curnock Est. NW1	A33
Cork St. W1	A49	Craven St. WC2	A51	**Cursitor St.**	**24**
Corlett St. NW1	A37	Craven Ter. W2	B36	Cursitor St. EC4	B42
Cornhill EC3	B44	Crawford Pass. EC1	A42	Curtain Rd. EC2	A44
Cornwall Gdns. SW7	A56	Crawford Pl. W1	B37		

Curzon Pl. W1	B49
Curzon St. W1	B49
Cuthbert St. W2	A37
Cutler St. E1	B45
Cut, The SE1	B52
Cynthia St. N1	A35
Cypress Pl. W1	A40
Dacre St. SW1	A60
Dallington St. EC1	A43
Dane St. WC1	B41
Dante Rd. SE11	B63
Danube St. SW3	B57
Daplyn St. E1	A45
D'arblay St. W1	B40
Dartmouth St. SW1	A60
Daventry St. NW1	A37
Davidge St. SE1	A63
David Ms. W1	A38
Davies Ms. W1	B39
Davies St.	**18**
Davies St. W1	B39
Deacon Way SE17	A63
Dean Bradley St. SW1	A61
Deanery St. W1	A49
Dean Farrar St. SW1	A60
Dean Ryle St. SW1	A61
Deans Ct. EC4	B43
Deans Ms. W1	B39
Dean Stanley St. SW1	A61
Dean St.	**20**
Dean St. W1	B40
Dean's Yd. SW1	A60
Dean Trench St. SW1	A61
Delamere Ter. W2	A36
Delancy St. NW1	A32
Delhi St. N1	A34
Delverton Rd. SE17	B63
Denbigh Pl. SW1	B60
Denbigh St. SW1	B60
Denman St. W1	A50
Denmark Pl. WC2	B40
Denmark St.	**20**
Denmark St. WC2	B40
Denning Clo. NW8	B30
Denny Cres. SE11	B62
Denny St. SE11	B62
Denyer St. SW3	B57
Derby Gro. SE1	B51
Derby St. W1	B49
Dering St.	**18**
Dering St. W1	B39
De Vere Gdns. W8	B46
Devonshire Clo. W1	A39
Devonshire Ms. S. W1	A39
Devonshire Ms. W1	A39
Devonshire Ms. W. W1	A39
Devonshire Pl. W1	A39
Devonshire Row EC2	B44
Devonshire Sq. EC2	B45
Devonshire St. W1	A39
Devonshire Ter. W2	B36
De Waldon St. W1	A39
Dewey Rd. N1	A35
Dial Wk. The W8	B46
Diana Pl. NW1	A39
Dickens Sq. SE1	A63
Dignum St. N1	A35
Disney Pl. SE1	B53
Disney St. SE1	B53
Distaff La. EC4	A53
Distin St. SE11	B62
Dock St. E1	A55
Dodson St. SE1	A62
Dolben St. SE1	B53
Dolland St. SE11	B62
Dombey St. WC1	A41
Dominion St. EC2	A44
Donegal St. N1	A35
Donne Pl. SW3	A57
Doon St. SE1	B52
Doric Way NW1	B33
Dorrington St. EC1	A42
Dorset Clo. NW1	A38
Dorset Ms. SW1	A59
Dorset Pl. SW1	B60
Doughty Ms. WC1	A41
Doughty St. WC1	A41
Douglas St. SW1	B60
Douro Pl. W8	B46
Dovehouse St. SW3	B57
Dove Ms. SW5	A56
Dover St.	**18**
Dover St. W1	A49
Dover Yd. W1	A49
Downgate Hl. EC4	A54
Downing St.	**22**
Downing St. SW1	B51
Down St. W1	B49
Doyce St. SE1	B53
Doyley St. SW1	A58
Drake St. WC1	A41
Draycott Av. SW3	A57
Draycott Pl. SW3	B58
Draycott Ter. SW1	B58
Drayton Gdns. SW10	B56
Druid St. SE1	B55
Drummond Cres. NW1	B33
Drummond St. NW1	B33
Drum St. E1	B45
Drury La.	**21**
Drury La. WC2	B41
Dryden St. WC2	B41
Duchess Ms. W1	A39
Duchess St. W1	B39
Duchy St. SE1	A52
Duck La. W1	A40
Dudmaston Ms. SW3	B57
Dufferin St. EC1	A44
Dufours Pl. W1	B40
Duke of Wellington Pl. SW1	B49
Duke of York St. SW1	A50
Duke's Ms. W1	B39
Duke's Pl. EC3	B45
Duke's Rd. WC1	B33
Duke St. Hl. SE1	B54
Duke St. SW1	A50
Duke St. W1	B39
Duncannon St. WC2	A51
Duncan St. N1	A35
Dunraven St. W1	A48
Dunstable Ms. W1	A39
Durham Ho. St. WC2	A51
Durham Pl. SW3	B58
Dyott St. WC1	B41
Dysart St. EC2	A44
Eagle Ct. EC1	A43
Eagle Pl. SW1	A50
Eagle St. WC1	B41
Eamont St. NW8	A30
Earlham St.	**20**
Earlham St. WC2	B41
Earl St. EC2	A44
Earnshaw St. WC2	B41
Easleys Ms. W1	B39
Eastbourne Ms. W2	B36
Eastbourne Ter. W2	B36
Eastcastle St. W1	B40

Eastcheap EC3	A54	
E. Harding St. EC4	B42	
Easton St. WC1	B35	
E. Poultry Av. EC1	A43	
E. Smithfield E1	A55	
East St. EC2	B44	
East St. SE17	B63	
E. Tenter St. E1	B45	
Eaton Clo. SW1	B58	
Eaton Gte.SW1	A58	
Eaton La. SW1	A58	
Eaton Ms. N. SW1	A59	
Eaton Ms. S. SW1	A59	
Eaton Ms. W. SW1	A59	
Eaton Pl. SW1	A58	
Eaton Row SW1	A59	
Eaton Sq. SW1	A58	
Eaton Ter. SW1	A58	
Eaton Ter. Ms. SW1	A58	
Ebor St. E1	A45	
Ebury Bri. Est. SW1	B59	
Ebury Bri. Rd. SW1	B59	
Ebury Bri. SW1	B59	
Ebury Ms. E. SW1	A59	
Ebury Ms. SW1	A59	
Ebury Sq. SW1	B59	
Ebury St. SW1	B59	
Eccleston Bri. SW1	A59	
Eccleston Ms. SW1	A59	
Eccleston Pl. SW1	B59	
Eccleston Sq. Ms. SW1	B59	
Eccleston Sq. SW1	B59	
Eccleston St. SW1	A59	
Eckersley St. E1	A45	
Eckford St. N1	A35	
Edgware Rd. NW8	A37	
Edinburgh Gte. SW1	B48	
Egerton Cres. Pl. SW3	A57	
Egerton Cres. SW3	A57	
Egerton Gdns. Ms. SW3	A57	
Egerton Gdns. SW3	A57	
Egerton Pl. SW3	A57	
Egerton Ter. SW3	A57	
Elba Pl. SE17	B63	
Elder St. E1	A45	
Eldon Rd. W8	A56	
Eldon St. EC2	B44	
Elephant & Castle SE1	B63	
Elephant Rd. SE17	B63	
Elizabeth St. SW1	A59	
Elliot's Row SE11	B63	
Ellis St. SW1	A58	
Elm Pk. Gdns. SW7	B57	
Elm Pk. La. SW3	B56	
Elm Pl. SW7	B57	
Elms Ms. W2	A47	
Elm St. WC1	A42	
Elm Tree Clo. NW8	B30	
Elm Tree Rd. NW8	B30	
Elnathan Ms. W9	A36	
Elvaston Ms. SW7	A56	
Elvaston Pl. SW7	A56	
Elverton St. SW1	A60	
Ely Pl. EC1	B42	
Elystan Pl. SW3	B57	
Elystan St. SW3	B57	
Elystan Wk. SW1	B57	
Embankment Pl. WC2	A51	
Emerald St. WC1	A41	
Emerson Pl. SE1	A53	
Emerson St. SE1	A53	
Emery Hl. St. SW1	A60	
Emperor's Gte. SW7	A56	
Endell St.	**21**	
Endell St. WC2	B41	
Endsleigh Gdns. WC1	B33	
Endsleigh Pl. WC1	A40	
Endsleigh St. WC1	B33	
Enford St. W1	A38	
English Gdns. SE1	B54	
Ennismore Gdns. Ms. SW7	A57	
Ennismore Gdns. SW7	B47	
Ennismore Ms. SW7	B47	
Ensor Ms. SW7	B56	
Epworth St. EC2	A44	
Erasmus St. SW1	B60	
Errol St. EC1	A44	
Essex Ct. EC4	B42	
Essex St.	**24**	
Essex St. WC2	B42	
Esterbrooke St. SW1	B60	
Ethel St. SE17	B63	
Euston Gro. NW1	B33	
Euston Rd. NW1	A39	
Euston Sq. NW1	B33	
Euston St. NW1	B33	
Evelyn Gdns. SW7	B56	
Evelyn Yd. W1	B40	
Everilda St. N1	A35	
Eversholt St. NW1	A33	
Everton Bldgs. NW1	B33	
Ewer St. SE1	B53	
Exeter St. WC2	A51	
Exhibition Rd. SW7	B47	
Exmouth Mkt. EC1	A42	
Exton St. SE1	B52	
Eyre Clo. SE1	A30	
Eyre St. Hl. EC1	A42	
Fairbolt St. SW7	A57	
Fairchild St. EC2	A45	
Fairlop Pl. NW8	B30	
Fair St. SE1	B55	
Falconberg Ms. W1	B40	
Falcon Clo. SE1	B53	
Falmouth Rd. SE1	A63	
Fann St. EC1	A44	
Farm St. W1	A49	
Farnham Pl. SE1	B53	
Farringdon Rd. EC1	B35	
Farringdon St. EC1	A42	
Farringdon St.	**25**	
Farringdon St. EC1	B42	
Fashion St. E1	B45	
Featherstone St. EC1	A44	
Fenchurch Av. EC3	A54	
Fenchurch Bldgs. EC3	B45	
Fenchurch Ct. EC3	A54	
Fenchurch St. EC3	A54	
Fenning St. SE1	B54	
Fernsby St. WC1	B35	
Fetter La.	**25**	
Fetter La. EC4	B42	
Field Ct. WC1	A42	
Field Pl. EC1	B35	
Fife Ter. N1	A35	
Finch La. EC3	B44	
Finchley Pl. NW8	A30	
Finchley Rd. NW8	A30	
Finck St. SE1	B52	
Finsbury Av. EC2	B44	
Finsbury Cir. EC2	B44	
Finsbury Mkt. EC2	A44	
Finsbury Pavement EC2	A44	
Finsbury Sq. EC2	B44	
Finsbury St. EC2	A44	
First St. SW3	A57	
Fisher Sq. WC1	B41	
Fisher St. Est. NW8	A37	
Fisherton St. NW8	A37	

Fish St. HI. EC3	A54	Galen Pl. WC1	B41	Glentworth St. NW1	A38
Fitzalan St. SE11	B62	Gambia St. SE1	B53	Globe St. SE1	A63
Fitzhardinge St. W1	B38	Ganton St. W1	B40	Gloucester Av. NW1	A32
Fitzmaurice Pl. W1	A49	Garbutt Pl. W1	A39	Gloucester Cres. NW1	A32
Fitzroy Ms. W1	A40	Garden Rd. NW8	B30	Gloucester Gdns. W2	B36
Fitzroy Sq. W1	A40	Garden Row SE1	A63	Gloucester Gte. NW1	A32
Fitzroy St. W1	A40	Gardners La. EC4	A53	Gloucester Ms. W2	B36
Flank St. E1	A55	Garlick HI. EC4	A53	Gloucester Ms. W. W2	B36
Flaxman Ter. WC1	B34	Garnault Ms. EC1	B35	Gloucester Pl. NW1	A38
Fleet La. EC4	B43	Garnault Pl. EC1	B35	Gloucester Pl. W1	A38
Fleet St. HI. E1	A45	Garrett St. EC1	A43	Gloucester Pl. W1	B38
Fleet St.	**25**	**Garrick St.**	**21**	Gloucester Rd. SW7	A56
Fleet St. WC2	B42	Garrick St. WC2	A51	Gloucester Sq. W2	B37
Fleur De Lis St. E1	A45	Gaspar Ms. SW5	A56	Gloucester St. SW1	B59
Flitcroft St. WC2	B40	Gateforth St. NW8	A37	Gloucester Ter. W2	B36
Flood St. SW3	B57	Gate St. WC2	B41	Gloucester Way EC1	B35
Floral St. WC2	A51	Gateways, The SW3	B58	Glynde Ms. SW3	A58
Flower & Dean St. E1	B45	Gatliff Rd. SW1	B59	Godfrey St. SW3	B57
Foley St. W1	A40	Gaunt St. SE1	A63	Godliman St. EC4	B43
Folgate St. E1	A45	Gayfere St. SW1	A61	Godson St. N1	A35
Fore Av. EC2	B44	Gaywood St. SE1	A63	Godwin Ct. NW1	A33
Fore St. EC2	B44	Gees Ct. W1	B39	Golden La. EC1	A43
Formosa St. W9	A36	Gee St. EC1	A43	Golden La. Est. EC1	A43
Forset St. W1	B38	George Inn Yd. SE1	B54	**Golden Sq.**	**19**
Fort St. E1	B45	George Row SE16	B55	Golden Sq. W1	A50
Fortune St. EC1	A43	George St. W1	B38	Goldford Pl. NW1	A37
Fosbury Ms. W2	A46	George Yd. W1	A49	Goldington Cres. NW1	A33
Foster La. EC2	B43	Gerald Rd. SW1	B59	Goldington St. NW1	A33
Foulis Ter. SW7	B57	Gerrard St. W1	A50	Goldman Clo. E2	A45
Fountain Ct. EC4	A52	Gerridge St. SE1	A62	Goodge Pl. W1	A40
Fourbert's Pl. W1	B40	Ghenies Ms. WC1	A40	Goodge St. W1	B40
Fournier St. E1	A45	Gibson Rd. SE11	B62	Goodman St. E1	A55
Frampton St. NW8	A37	Gilbert Pl. WC1	B41	Goodman's Yd. E1	A55
Francis St. SW1	A60	Gilbert Rd. SE11	B62	Goods Way NW1	A34
Franklin's Row SW3	B58	Gilbert St. W1	B39	Goodwins Ct. WC2	A51
Frazier St. SE1	B52	Gildea St. W1	A39	Goose Yd. EC1	B35
Frederick Clo. W2	B38	Giles Cir. W1	B40	Gordon Sq. WC1	A40
Frederick St. WC1	B34	Gillingham Ms. SW1	A59	Gordon St. WC1	B33
Friar St. EC4	B43	Gillingham Row SW1	B59	Gore St. SW7	A56
Friday St. EC4	A53	Gillingham St. SW1	B59	Goring St. EC3	B45
Frith St.	**20**	Gilston Rd. SW10	B56	Gosfield St. W1	A39
Frith St. W1	B40	Giltspur St. EC1	B43	Goslett Yd. WC2	B40
Frying Pan All. E1	B45	Gladstone St. SE1	A62	Goswell Rd. EC1	B35
Fulham Rd. SW3	B56	Glasgow Ter. SW1	B59	**Gough Sq.**	**25**
Fulton Ms. W2	A46	Glasshill St. SE1	B53	Gough Sq. EC4	B42
Fulwood Pl. WC1	B42	**Glasshouse St.**	**19**	Gough St. WC1	B42
Furnival St.	**25**	Glasshouse St. W1	A50	Goulston St. E1	B45
Furnival St. EC4	B42	Glasshouse Wk. SE11	B61	Gower Ct. WC1	A40
Fynes St. SW1	A60	Glasshouse Yd. EC1	A43	Gower Ms. WC1	A40
Gage St. WC1	A41	Gledhow Gdns. SW5	B56	Gower Pl. WC1	A40
Gainsford St. SE1	B55	Glendower Pl. SW7	A57	Gower St. WC1	A40

Gracechurch St. EC3	A54	
Grafton Ms. W1	A40	
Grafton Pl. NW1	B33	
Grafton St.	**18**	
Grafton St. W1	A49	
Grafton Way W1	A40	
Graham Ter. SW3	B58	
Granby St. E2	A45	
Granby Ter. NW1	B33	
Grand Av. EC1	A43	
Grange Ct. WC2	B42	
Grantham Pl. W1	B49	
Grant St. N1	A35	
Granville Pl. W1	B38	
Granville Sq. WC1	B35	
Granville St. WC1	B35	
Grape St. WC2	B41	
Gravel La. E1	B45	
Gray's Inn Pl. WC1	A42	
Gray's Inn Rd. WC1	B34	
Gray's Inn Rd. WC1	A42	
Gray's Inn Sq. WC1	A42	
Gray St. SE1	B52	
Gt. Castle St. W1	B39	
Gt. Central St. NW1	A38	
Gt. Chapel St. W1	B40	
Gt. College St. SW1	A61	
Gt. Cumberland Ms. W1	B38	
Gt. Cumberland Pl. W1	B38	
Gt. Dover St. SE1	B53	
Gt. Eastern St. EC2	A44	
Gt. George St. SW1	B50	
Gt. Guildford St. SE1	B53	
Gt. James St. WC1	A41	
Gt. Marlborough St.	**19**	
Gt. Marlborough St. W1	B40	
Gt. Newport St.	**20**	
Gt. Newport St. WC2	A51	
Gt. New St. EC4	B42	
Gt. Ormond St. WC1	A41	
Gt. Percy St. WC1	B35	
Gt. Peter St. SW1	A60	
Gt. Portland St.	**19**	
Gt. Portland St. W1	A39	
Gt. Pulteney St. W1	B40	
Gt. Queen St.	**21**	
Gt. Queen St. WC2	B41	
Gt. Russell St.	**20**	
Gt. Russell St. WC1	B40	
Gt. St. Helens EC3	B44	
Gt. St. Thomas Apostle EC4	A53	
Gt. Scotland Yard	**23**	
Gt. Scotland Yd. SW1	B51	
Gt. Smith St. SW1	A60	
Gt. Suffolk St. SE1	B53	
Gt. Sutton St. EC1	A43	
Gt. Swan Alley EC2	B44	
Gt. Tichfield St.	**19**	
Gt. Tichfield St. W1	A39	
Gt. Tower St. EC3	A54	
Gt. Turnstile WC2	B42	
Gt. Winchester St. EC2	B44	
Greek St.	**20**	
Greek St. W1	B40	
Greenberry St. NW8	A30	
Greencoat Pl. SW1	A60	
Greencoat Row SW1	A60	
Green Dragon Yd. E1	B45	
Greenhills Rents EC1	A43	
Green St. W1	A48	
Green Ter. EC1	B35	
Greenwell St. W1	A39	
Greet St. SE1	B52	
Grenville Pl. SW7	A56	
Grenville St. WC1	A41	
Gresham St. EC2	B43	
Gresse St. W1	B40	
Greville St. EC1	B42	
Greycoat Pl. SW1	A60	
Greycoat St. SW1	A60	
Grey Eagle St. E1	A45	
Grimsby St. E2	A45	
Grindal St. SE1	B52	
Groom Pl. SW1	B48	
Grosvenor Cres. SW1	B48	
Grosvenor Cres. Ms. SW1	B48	
Grosvenor Est. SW1	A60	
Grosvenor Gdns. SW1	A59	
Grosvenor Gdns. Ms. N. SW1	A59	
Grosvenor Hl. W1	A49	
Grosvenor Pl. SW1	B49	
Grosvenor Sq.	**18**	
Grosvenor Sq. W1	A49	
Grosvenor St.	**18**	
Grosvenor St. W1	A49	
Grove Ct. NW8	B30	
Grove End Gdns. NW8	A30	
Grove End Rd. NW8	B30	
Grove Gdns. NW8	B30	
Guildhall Bldgs. EC2	B44	
Guildhall Yd. EC2	B44	
Guildhouse St. SW1	B59	
Guilford Pl. WC1	A41	
Guilford St. WC1	A41	
Guinness Bldgs. SE11	B63	
Guinness Bldgs. SW3	B58	
Gundulf St. SE11	B62	
Gunthorpe St. E1	B45	
Gutter La. EC2	B43	
Guy St. SE1	B54	
Gwynne Pl. WC1	B35	
Habet Rd. W2	A37	
Half Moon Pass E1	B45	
Half Moon St. W1	A49	
Halkin Arc. SW1	A58	
Halkin Pl. SW1	A58	
Halkin St. SW1	A58	
Hallam St. W1	A39	
Hallfield Est. W2	B36	
Hall Gte. NW8	B30	
Hall Pl. W2	A37	
Halsey St. SW3	A58	
Hamilton Pl. W1	B49	
Hamilton Sq. SE1	B54	
Hampden Clo. NW1	A33	
Hampden Gurney Pl. W1	B38	
Hampstead Rd. NW1	A33	
Hampton St. SE17	B63	
Hanbury St. E1	A45	
Hand Ct. WC1	B42	
Handel St. WC1	A41	
Hankey Pl. SE1	B54	
Hanover Gte. NW1	B31	
Hanover Gte. Mans. NW1	B31	
Hanover Ms. NW1	B31	
Hanover Sq.	**18**	
Hanover Sq. W1	B39	
Hanover Ter. NW1	B31	
Hans Cres. SW1	B48	
Hanson St. W1	A40	
Hans Pl. SW1	A58	
Hans Rd. SW3	A58	
Hans St. SW1	A58	
Hanway Pl. W1	B40	
Hanway St. W1	B40	
Harcourt St. W1	A38	

Harcourt Ter. SW10	B56
Hardwick St. EC1	B35
Hardwidge St. SE1	B54
Hare Pl. EC4	B42
Harewood Av. NW1	A38
Harewood Pl. W1	B39
Harewood Row NW1	A38
Harley Gdns. SW10	B56
Harley Pl. W1	B39
Harley St. W1	A39
Harp Alley EC4	B42
Harper Rd. SE1	A63
Harp La. EC3	A54
Harpur St. WC1	A41
Harriet St. SW1	B48
Harriet Wk. SW1	B48
Harrington Gdns. SW7	B56
Harrington Rd. SW7	B56
Harrington Sq. NW1	A33
Harrington St. NW1	B33
Harrison St. WC1	B34
Harrowby St. W1	B38
Harrow Pl. E1	B45
Hart St. EC3	A55
Hasker St. SW3	A58
Hastings St. WC1	B34
Hatfield St. SE1	A52
Hatherley Gro. W2	B36
Hatherley St. SW1	B60
Hatton Gdn. EC1	A42
Hatton Pl. EC1	A42
Hatton Row NW8	A37
Hatton St. NW8	A37
Hatton Wall EC1	A42
Haunch Of Venison Yd.	B39
W1	
Havelock St. N1	A34
Haydon St. EC3	A55
Hayes Pl. NW1	A38
Hay Hl. W1	A49
Hayles St. SE11	B63
Haymarket	**22**
Haymarket SW1	A50
Hayne St. EC1	A43
Hays La. SE1	B54
Hays Ms. W1	A49
Haywards Pl. EC1	A43
Headfort Pl. SW1	B49
Hearn St. EC2	A44
Heathcote St. WC1	B34
Heddon St. W1	A50

Helmet Row EC1	A43
Hemingford Rd. N1	A35
Hemus Pl. SW3	B57
Henderson Dr. NW8	B30
Heneage La. EC3	B45
Heneage St. E1	B45
Henrietta Ms. WC1	B34
Henrietta Pl.	**18**
Henrietta Pl. W1	B39
Henrietta St.	**21**
Henrietta St. WC2	A51
Hensridge Pl. NW8	A30
Herbal Hl. EC1	A42
Herbert Cres. SW1	A58
Herbrand St. WC1	A41
Hercules Rd. SE1	A62
Hereford Sq. SW7	B56
Hermes St. N1	A35
Herrick St. SW1	B60
Hertford Pl. W1	A40
Hertford St. W1	B49
Hesper Ms. SW5	B56
Heygate St. SE17	B63
Hide Pl. SW1	B60
High Holborn	**21**
High Holborn WC1	B41
High Timber St. EC4	A53
Hills Pl. W1	B40
Hill St.	**18**
Hill St. W1	A49
Hind Ct.	**25**
Hind Ct. EC4	B42
Hinde St. W1	B39
Hobart Pl. SW1	A59
Holbein Ms. SW3	B58
Holbein Pl. SW1	B58
Holborn WC1	B42
Holborn Cir. EC1	B42
Holborn Viaduct	**25**
Holborn Viaduct EC1	B42
Holford Pl. WC1	B35
Holland St. SE1	A53
Hollen St. W1	B40
Holles St.	**18**
Holles St. W1	B39
Holyoake Rd. SE11	B63
Holyrood St. SE1	B54
Holywell La. EC2	A45
Holywell Row EC2	A44
Homer Row W1	A37
Homer St. W1	A38

Honduras St. EC1	A43
Honey La. EC2	B43
Hoopers Ct. SW3	B48
Hooper St. E1	A55
Hopetown St. E1	B45
Hopkins St. W1	B40
Hopton St. SE1	A53
Horseferry Rd. SW1	A60
Horse Guards Av.	**23**
Horse Guards Av. SW1	B51
Horse Guards Rd. SW1	B50
Horselydown La. SE1	B55
Hosier La. EC1	B43
Houghton St. WC2	B41
Houndsditch EC3	B44
Howick Pl. SW1	A60
Howland Ms. E. W1	A40
Howland Ms. W. W1	A40
Howland St. W1	A40
Howley Pl. W2	A36
Hudson Pl. SW1	A59
Huggin Hl. EC4	A53
Hugh Ms. SW1`	B59
Hugh St. SW1	B59
Hungerford Bri.	**23**
Hunter St. WC1	B34
Huntley St. WC1	A40
Hunton St. E1	A45
Huntsworth Ms. NW1	A38
Hyde Park Corner W1	B49
Hyde Pk. Cres. W2	B37
Hyde Pk. Gdns. W2	A47
Hyde Pk. Gdns. W2	B37
Hyde Pk. Gdns. Ms. W2	B37
Hyde Pk. Gte. SW7	B46
Hyde Pk. Gte. Ms.	B46
SW7	
Hyde Pk. Mans. NW1	A37
Hyde Pk. Pl. W2	B38
Hyde Pk. Sq. W2	B37
Hyde Pk. St. W2	B37
Idol La. EC3	A54
Iliffe St. SE17	B63
Iliffe Yd. SE17	B63
Imperial Institute Rd.	A56
SW7	
India St. EC3	A55
Ingestre Pl. W1	B40
Inglebert St. EC1	B35
Inner Circle NW1	B31
Insurance St. WC1	B35

Inverness Ms. W2	B36	Kendal St. W2	B37	King St. EC2	B44

Inverness Ms. W2 — B36
Inverness Pl. W2 — A46
Inverness Ter. W2 — B36
Ireland Yd. EC4 — B43
Ironmonger La. EC2 — B44
Irving St. — 20
Irving St. WC2 — A50
Isabella St. SE1 — B52
Islington High St. N1 — A35
Ives St. SW3 — B57
Ixworth Pl. SW3 — B57
Jacobs Well Pl. W1 — B39
James St. — 21
James St. W1 — B39
James St. WC2 — B41
Jay Ms. SW7 — B46
Jermyn St. — 19
Jermyn St. SW1 — A50
Jerome Cres. NW8 — B30
Jerome St. E1 — A45
Jerusalem Pass. EC1 — A43
Jewry St. EC3 — B45
Joan St. SE1 — B52
Jockey's Flds. WC1 — A42
Johanna St. SE1 — B52
John Adam St. — 23
John Adam St. WC2 — A51
John Carpenter St. — 25
John Carpenter St. EC4 — A52
John Felton Rd. SE16 — B55
John Fisher St. E1 — A55
John Islip St. SW1 — B60
John Prince's St. — 18
John Prince's St. W1 — B39
John's Ms. WC1 — A42
Johnsons Pl. SW1 — B60
John St. WC1 — A42
Joiner St. SE1 — B54
Jonathan St. SE11 — B61
Jones St. W1 — A49
Jubilee Pl. SW3 — B57
Judd St. WC1 — B34
Junction Ms. W2 — B37
Juxon St. SE11 — B61
Kean St. WC2 — B41
Keeley St. WC2 — B41
Kelso Pl. W8 — A56
Kemble St. — 21
Kemble St. WC2 — B41
Kempsford Rd. SE11 — B62
Kendall Pl. W1 — B38

Kendal St. W2 — B37
Kendrick Ms. SW7 — A57
Kennings Way SE11 — B62
Kennington La. SE11 — B62
Kennington Rd. SE1 — A62
Kenrick Pl. W1 — B39
Kensington Ct. W8 — B46
Kensington Ct. Pl. W8 — A56
Kensington Gdns. Sq. W2 — B36
Kensington Gte. W8 — A56
Kensington Gore SW7 — B46
Kensington Pal. Gdns. W8 — B46
Kensington Rd. W8 — B46
Kensington Sq. W8 — B46
Kenton St. WC1 — B34
Kent Pass NW1 — B31
Kent Ter. NW1 — B31
Keppel Row SE1 — B53
Keppel St. WC1 — A40
Ker St. E2 — A45
Keyston Cres. N1 — A34
Keyworth St. SE1 — A63
Kiffen St. EC2 — A44
Killick St. N1 — A34
King & Queen St. SE17 — B63
King Charles St. SW1 — B51
King Edward St. EC1 — B43
King Edward Wk. SE1 — A62
King James St. SE1 — A63
King John Ct. EC2 — A45
Kingly Ct. W1 — A50
Kingly St. — 19
Kingly St. W1 — A50
Kings Arms Yd. EC2 — B44
King's Bench St. SE1 — B53
King's Bench Wk. EC4 — A52
Kingscote St. EC4 — A53
King's Cross Rd. WC1 — B34
Kingsley Ms. W8 — A56
King's Ms. WC1 — A42
Kingsmill Ter. NW8 — A30
Kings Pl. SE1 — A63
King's Rd. SW1 — B60
King's Scholar's Pass. SW1 — A60
King's Ter. NW1 — A33
King St. — 21

King St. EC2 — B44
King St. SW1 — B50
King St. WC2 — A51
Kingsway — 21
Kingsway WC2 — B41
King William St. EC4 — B44
Kinnerton Pl. N. SW1 — B48
Kinnerton Pl. S. SW1 — B48
Kinnerton St. SW1 — B48
Kipling Est. SE1 — B54
Kipling St. SE1 — B54
Kirby Gro. SE1 — B54
Kirby St. EC1 — A42
Knightrider St. EC4 — A53
Knightsbridge SW7 — B47
Knightsbridge Clo. SW1 — B48
Knox St. W1 — A38
Kynance Ms. SW7 — A56
Kynance Pl. SW7 — A56
Lackington St. EC2 — A44
Lafone St. SE1 — B55
Lambeth High St. SE1 — B61
Lambeth Ms. SE11 — B61
Lambeth Palace Rd. SE1 — A61
Lambeth Rd. SE1 — A61
Lambeth St. E1 — B45
Lambeth Wk. SE11 — B61
Lambs Bldgs. EC1 — A44
Lambs Conduit Pass. WC1 — A41
Lambs Conduit St. WC1 — A41
Lambs Pass. EC1 — A44
Lamb St. E1 — A45
Lamlash St. SE11 — A63
Lanark Pl. W9 — A36
Lancaster Ct. W2 — A46
Lancaster Gte. W2 — A46
Lancaster Ms. W2 — B36
Lancaster Pl. — 23
Lancaster Pl. WC2 — A51
Lancaster St. SE1 — A53
Lancaster Ter. W2 — A47
Lancelot Pl. SW7 — B48
Lancing St. NW1 — B33
Landon Pl. SW1 — A58
Lanfranc St. SE1 — A62
Langdon Pl. SW1 — A58
Langford Ct. NW8 — A30

Langford Pl. NW8	A30	Leveret St. SW3	B57	Liverpool St. EC2	B44
Langham Pl. W1	B39	Lewisham St. SW1	B50	Livonia St. W1	B40
Langham St. W1	B39	Lewis Trust Bldgs. SW3	B57	Lloyd Baker St. WC1	B35
Langley St. WC2	B41	Lexham Gdns. W8	A56	Lloyds Av. EC3	B44
Langton Cl. WC1	B35	Lexham Wk. W8	A56	Lloyd Sq. WC1	B35
Lansdowne Row W1	A49	**Lexington St.**	**19**	Lloyd's Row EC1	B35
Lansdowne Ter. WC1	A41	Lexington St. W1	B40	Lloyd St. WC1	B35
Lant St. SE1	B53	Leyden St. E1	B45	Lockyer St. SE1	B54
Larcom St. SE17	B63	Library St. SE1	A63	Lodge Rd. NW8	B30
Laud St. SE11	B61	Ligonier St. E2	A45	Lolesworth St. E1	B45
Launcelot St. SE1	B52	Lilac St. W8	B61	Lollard Pl. SE11	B62
Launceston Pl. W8	A56	Lilestone Est. NW8	A37	Lollard St. SE11	B62
Laverton Pl. SW5	B56	Lilestone St. NW8	A37	Loman St. SE1	B53
Lavina Gro. N1	A34	Lillington Gdns. Est.		Lombard La. EC4	B42
Lavington St. SE1	B53	SW1	B60	Lombard St. EC3	B44
Lawrence La. EC2	B43	Lime St. EC3	A54	London Bridge St. SE1	B54
Lawrence Pountney Hl.	A54	**Lincoln's Inn Fields**	**24**	London Ms. W2	B37
EC4		Lincoln's Inn Flds. WC2	B41	London Rd. SE1	A63
Lawrence Pountney La.	A54	Lincoln St. SW3	B58	London St. EC3	A55
EC4		Lindsey St. EC1	A43	London St. W2	B37
Lawrence St. NW1	A34	Linhope St. NW1	A38	London Wall EC2	B43
Laxton Pl. NW1	B32	Liplington Pl. NW1	A33	**Long Acre**	**21**
Laystall St. EC1	A42	**Lisle St.**	**20**	Long Acre WC2	A51
Layton Rd. N1	A35	Lisle St. WC2	A50	Longford St. NW1	B32
Leadenhall Pl. EC3	B44	Lisson Gro. NW8	B30	Long La. EC1	A43
Leadenhall St. EC3	B44	Lisson St. NW1	A37	Long La. SE1	B54
Leake Ct. SE1	B52	Litchfield St. WC2	B41	Longmoor Ct. SW1	B60
Leake St. SE1	B52	Lit. Albany St. NW1	B32	Longville Rd. SE11	B63
Leather La. EC1	A42	Lit. Argyll St. W1	B40	Long Yd. WC1	A41
Leathermarket St. SE1	B54	Lit. Boltons, The	B56	Lord Hills Rd. W2	A36
Lecky St. SW7	B57	SW10		Lord North St. SW1	A61
Leeke St. WC1	B34	Lit. Britain EC1	B43	Lorenzo St. WC1	B34
Lees Pl. W1	A48	Lit. Chester St. SW1	A59	Lothbury EC2	B44
Leicester Ct. WC2	A50	Lit. College St. SW1	A61	Loudoun Rd. NW8	A30
Leicester Sq	**20**	Lit. Dorrit Ct. SE1	B53	Loughborough St.	B62
Leicester Sq. WC2	A50	Lit. Edward St. NW1	B32	SE11	
Leicester St. WC2	A50	Lit. George St. SW1	B51	Lovat La. EC3	A54
Leigh Hunt St. SE1	B53	Lit. Marlborough St.	B40	Love La. EC2	B43
Leigh St. WC1	B34	W1		Lwr. Belgrave St. SW1	A59
Leinster Gdns. W2	B36	Lit. Newport St. WC2	A50	Lwr. Grosvenor Pl.	A59
Leinster Ms. W2	A46	Lit. New St. EC4	B42	SW1	
Leinster Pl. W2	B36	Lit. Portland St. N1	B39	Lwr. James St. W1	A50
Leinster Ter. W2	A46	Lit. Russell St. WC1	B41	Lwr. John St. W1	A50
Leman St. E2	B45	Lit. St. James's St. SW1	B50	Lwr. Marsh SE1	B52
Lennox Gdns. SW1	A58	Lit. Smith St. SW1	A60	Lwr. Newport St. WC2	A50
Lennox Gdns. Ms.	A58	Lit. Somerset St. E1	B45	Lwr. Sloane St. SW1	B58
SW1		Lit. Tichfield St. W1	B39	Lwr. Thames St. EC3	A54
Lenthall Pl. SW7	A56	Lit. Trinity La. EC4	A54	Lowndes Clo. SW1	A58
Leonard's Ter. SW3	B58	Lit. Turnstile St. WC2	B41	Lowndes Pl. SW1	A58
Leonard St. EC2	A44	Liverpool Rd. N1	A35	Lowndes Sq. SW1	B48
Leo Yd. EC1	A43			Lowndes St. SW1	A58

Loxham St. WC1	B34	Mansfield Ms. W1	A39	Matilda St. N1	A35
Lucan Pl. SW3	B57	Mansfield St. W1	A39	Mathew Parker St.	A60
Ludgate Circus	**25**	Mansion Ho. St. EC2	B44	SW1	
Ludgate Cir. EC4	B43	Manson Ms. SW7	B56	Maunsel St. SW1	A60
Ludgate Hill	**25**	Manson Pl. SW7	B56	Mayfair Pl. W1	A49
Ludgate Hi. EC4	B43	Mantell St. N1	A35	Maygood St. N1	A35
Ludgate Sq. EC4	B43	Maple Pl. W1	A40	Mays Ct. WC2	A51
Luke St. EC2	A44	Maple St. W1	A40	Mcleods Ms. SW7	A56
Lumley St. W1	B39	Macquire St. SE1	B55	Meadow Row SE1	A62
Lupus St. SW1	B59	Marble Arch W1	B38	Meadow Row SE1	A63
Luton St. NW8	A37	Margery St. WC1	B35	Meard St. W1	B40
Luxborough St. W1	A38	**Margaret St.**	**18**	Mecklenburgh Pl. WC1	A41
Lyall Ms. SW1	A58	Margaret St. W1	B39	Mecklenburgh Sq. WC1	B34
Lyall Ms. W. SW1	A58	Margery St. WC1	B35	Medburn St. NW1	A33
Lyall St. SW1	A58	Market Ms. W1	B49	Medcalf Pl. EC1	B35
Lygon Pl. SW1	A59	Market Pl. W1	B39	Medway St. SW1	A60
Lyons Pl. NW8	A37	Markham Sq. SW3	B58	Melbourne Pl. WC2	B42
Mableton Pl. WC1	B34	Markham St. SW3	B58	Melbury Ter. NW1	A38
Macclesfield Bri. NW8	A31	Mark La. EC3	A55	Melcombe Pl. NW1	A38
Macclesfield St. W1	A50	Mark St. EC2	A44	Melcombe St. NW1	A38
Macfarren Pl. NW1	A39	Marlborough All. SE1	A52	Melior St. SE1	B54
Mackennal St. NW8	A30	Marlborough Bldgs.		Melton Ct. SW7	B57
Macklin St. WC2	B41	SW3		Melton St. NW1	B33
Mackworth St. NW1	B33	Marlborough Clo.	B63	Mepham St. SE1	B52
Maddox St.	**18**	SE17		Mercer St. WC2	B41
Maddox St. W1	A49	Marlborough Ct. W1	B40	Meredith St. EC1	B35
Magdalen St. SE1	B54	Marlborough Hi. NW8	A30	Merlin St. WC1	B35
Magpie All. EC4	B42	Marlborough Rd. SW1	B50	Mermaid Ct. SE1	B54
Maguire St. SE1	B55	Marlborough Rd. SW3	B57	Merrick Sq. SE1	A63
Maida Av. W2	A36	Marloes, The NW8	A30	Merritts Bldgs. EC2	A44
Maiden La.	**21**	Marshall Gdns. SE1	A63	Meymott St. SE1	B52
Maiden La. WC2	A51	Marshall St. W1	B40	Middlesex St. E1	B45
Maidstone Bldgs. SE1	B53	Marshalsea Rd. SE1	B53	Middle St. EC1	A44
Makins St. SW3	B57	Marsham St. SW1	A60	**Middle Temple La.**	**24**
Malet Pl. WC1	A40	Martin La. EC4	A54	Middle Temple La. EC4	B42
Malet St. WC1	A40	Martlett Ct. WC2	B41	Middleton Pass. EC1	B35
Mallory St. NW8	A37	Mart St. WC2	B41	Midford Pl. W1	A40
Mallow St. EC1	A44	Marylebone Cir. NW1	A38	Midhope St. WC1	B34
Mall, The	**22**	Marylebone High St.	B39	Midland Rd. NW1	A34
Mall, The SW1	B50	W1		Milborne Gro. SW10	B56
Maltravers St. WC2	A52	**Marylebone La.**	**18**	Milcote St. SE1	A63
Malvern Ct. SW7	A57	Marylebone La. W1	B39	Miles La. EC4	A54
Manchester Sq. W1	A38	Marylebone Ms. W1	B39	Miles Pl. NW1	A37
Manchester St. W1	A38	Marylebone Pass. W1	B39	Milford La. WC2	A52
Mandeville Hos. N1	A35	Marylebone Rd. NW1	A38	Milk St. EC2	B43
Mandeville Pl. W1	B39	Marylebone St. W1	A39	Millbank SW1	A61
Manette St. W1	B40	Marylee Way SE11	B62	Miller St. NW1	A33
Manningtree St. E1	B45	Mary Ter. NW1	A32	Millmans St. WC1	A41
Manor Pl. SE17	B63	Mason's Arms Ms. W1	B39	Mill St. SE1	B55
Manresa Rd. SW3	B57	Masons Av. EC2	B44	Mill St. W1	B39
Mansell St. E1	B45	Mason St. SW1	A50	Milner St. SW3	A58

Milroy Wk. SE1	A52
Milton Ct. EC2	A44
Milton St. EC2	A44
Mincing La. EC3	A54
Minera Ms. SW1	A58
Minories EC3	B45
Mint St. SE1	B53
Mitchell St. EC1	A43
Mitre Ct. EC2	B43
Mitre Rd. SE1	B52
Mitre St. EC3	B45
Model Bldgs. WC1	B35
Molyneux St. W1	B38
Monck St. SW1	A60
Monkton St. SE11	B62
Monkwell Sq. EC2	B43
Monmouth St.	**20**
Monmouth St. WC2	B41
Montague Clo. SE1	A54
Montague Pl. WC1	B41
Montague St. WC1	A41
Montagu Ms. N. W1	A38
Montagu Ms. S. W1	B38
Montagu Ms. W. W1	B38
Montagu Pl. W1	B38
Montagu Sq. W1	B38
Montagu St. W1	B38
Montford St. EC3	B45
Montpelier Ms. SW7	A58
Montpelier Pl. SW7	A57
Montpelier Sq. SW7	B47
Montpelier St. SW7	B47
Montpelier Ter. SW7	B47
Montpelier Wk. SW7	B47
Montreal Pl. WC2	A51
Montrose Pl. SW1	B49
Monument St. EC3	A54
Moon St. N1	A35
Moore St. SW3	A58
Moorfields EC2	B44
Moorgate EC2	B44
Moor La. EC2	A44
Moor La. EC2	B44
Moor St. W1	B40
Morecambe St. SE17	B63
Moreton Pl. SW1	B60
Moreton St. SW1	B60
Moreton Ter. SW1	B60
Morgan's La. SE1	B54
Morley St. SE1	A62
Mornington Cres. NW1	A33
Mornington Pl. NW1	A32
Mornington St. NW1	A32
Mornington Ter. NW1	A32
Morocco St. SE1	B54
Morpeth Ter. SW1	A60
Mortimer Mkt. WC1	A40
Mortimer St. W1	B39
Morton Pl. SE1	A62
Morwell St. WC1	B40
Moscow Pl. W2	B36
Mossop St. SW3	B57
Motcomb St. SW1	A58
Mount Pleasant WC1	A42
Mount Row W1	A49
Mount St.	**18**
Mount St. W1	A48
Moxon St. W1	A39
Mulready St. NW8	A37
Munster Sq. NW1	B32
Munton Rd. SE17	B63
Muriel St. N1	A35
Murphy St. SE1	A62
Muscovy St. EC3	A55
Museum St. WC1	B41
Myddelton Pass. EC1	B35
Myddelton Sq. EC1	B35
Myddelton St. EC1	B35
Mylne St. EC1	B35
Nash St. NW1	B32
Nassau St. W1	B40
Neal St.	**21**
Neal St. WC2	B41
Neathouse Clo. SW1	A59
Nelson Sq. SE1	B53
Netley St. NW1	B33
Neville Clo. WC1	A34
Neville Ct. NW8	A30
Neville St. SW7	B57
Neville Ter. SW7	B57
New Bond St.	**18**
New Bond St. W1	B39
New Bridge St.	**25**
New Bridge St. EC4	B43
New Broad St. EC2	B44
Newburgh St. W1	B40
New Burlington Pl. W1	A50
New Burlington St.	**19**
New Burlington St. W1	A50
Newburn St. SE11	B62
Newbury St. EC1	A43
Newcastle Ct. EC4	B43
Newcastle Pl. W2	A37
New Cavendish St. W1	B39
New Change EC4	B43
Newcomen St. SE1	B54
New Compton St.	**20**
New Compton St. WC2	B41
New Ct. WC2	B42
Newcourt St. NW8	A30
New Coventry St. W1	A50
New Fetter La. EC4	B42
Newgate St. EC1	B43
New Goulston St. E1	B45
Newington Butts SE11	B63
Newington Causeway SE1	A63
New Inn St. EC2	A45
New Inn Yd. EC2	A45
New Kent Rd. SE1	A63
Newman Pass. W1	B40
Newmans Row WC2	B42
Newman St. W1	B40
Newman Yd. W1	B40
Newnham St. E1	B45
Newnman Ter. SE1	A62
New North Pl. EC2	A44
New North St. WC1	A41
New Oxford St.	**20**
New Oxford St. WC1	B40
New Palace Yd. SW1	B51
Newport Ct. WC2	A50
Newport Pl. WC2	A50
Newport St. SE11	B61
Newport St. WC2	A50
New Quebec St. W1	B38
New Row WC2	A51
New St. Sq. EC4	B42
New Sq. WC2	B42
New St. EC2	B45
Newton St. WC2	B41
New Wharf N1	A34
Nicholas La. EC4	A54
Nicolson St. SE1	B53
Noble St. EC2	B43
Noel St. W1	B40
Norfolk Cres. W2	B37
Norfolk Pl. W2	A37
Norfolk Rd. NW8	A30
Norfolk Row SE11	A61
Norfolk Sq. W2	B37
Norris St. SW1	A50

Name	Ref	Name	Ref	Name	Ref
Northampton Bldgs. EC1	B35	**Old Compton St.**	**20**	Outer Circle NW1	A31
Northampton Rd. EC1	A42	Old Compton St. W1	B40	Outer Circle NW1	A32
North Audley St. W1	B38	Old Gloucester St. WC1	A41	Outram St. NW1	A34
North Bank NW8	B30	Old Jewry EC2	B44	Oval Rd. NW1	A32
Northburgh St. EC1	A43	Old Marylebone Rd. NW1	B37	Ovington Gdns. SW3	A57
North Ct. W1	A40	Old Montague St. E1	B45	Ovington Ms. SW3	A57
North Cres. WC1	A40	Old Nichol St. E2	A45	Ovington Sq. SW3	A58
Northdown St. N1	A34	Old North St. WC1	A41	Ovington St. SW3	A58
North Gower St. NW1	B33	Old Palace Yd. SW1	A61	Owens Row EC1	B35
Northington St. WC1	A41	Old Paradise St. SE11	A61	Owen St. EC1	B35
North Ms. WC1	A42	Old Pk. La. W1	A49	Oxendon St. SW1	A50
North Ride W2	A47	Old Pye St. SW1	A60	**Oxford Circus**	**19**
North Row W1	B38	Old Quebec St. W1	B38	Oxford Cir. W1	B39
North Tenter St. E1	B45	Old Queen St. SW1	B50	Oxford Sq. W2	B37
North Ter. SW3	A57	Old Seacoal La. EC4	B43	**Oxford St.**	**18**
Northumberland All. EC3	B45	Old Sq. WC2	B42	Oxford St. W1	B38
Northumberland Av.	**23**	Old St. EC1	A43	Paddington Grn. W2	A37
Northumberland Av. WC2	A51	Olivers Yd. EC2	A44	Paddington St. W1	A38
Northumberland St. WC2	A51	Olympia Yd. W2	A46	Page St. SW1	A60
Northwest Pl. N1	A35	O'meara St. SE1	B53	Pakenham St. WC1	B35
North Wharf Rd. W2	A37	Omega Pl. N1	B34	Palace Av. W8	B46
Northwick Clo. NW8	B30	Onslow Gdns. SW7	B56	Palace Gte. W8	B46
Northwick Ter. NW8	B30	Onslow Ms. W. SW7	B57	Palace St. SW1	A59
Norton Folgate E1	A45	Onslow Sq. SW7	B57	Pallitt Dr. NW8	B30
Norwich St. EC4	B42	Onslow St. EC1	A42	**Pall Mall**	**22**
Nott Ct. W2	B41	Ontario St. SE1	A63	Pall Mall SW1	B50
Nottingham Pl. W1	A38	Opal St. SE11	B62	**Pall Mall East**	**22**
Nottingham St. W1	A38	Orange St. WC2	A50	Pall Mall E. SW1	A50
Nutford Pl. W1	B38	Orchardson St. NW8	A37	Pall Mall Pl. SW1	B50
Oakden St. SE11	B62	Orchard St. W1	B38	Palmer St. SW1	A60
Oakley Sq. NW1	A33	Orde Hall St. WC1	A41	Pancras La. EC4	B44
Oak Tree Rd. NW8	B30	Ordnance Hl. NW8	A30	Pancras Rd. NW1	A33
Oat La. EC2	B43	Orient St. SE11	A62	**Panton St.**	**20**
Occupation Rd. SE17	B63	Orme Ct. W2	A46	Panton St. SW1	A50
Ogle St. W1	A40	Orme La. W2	A46	Panyer Alley EC4	B43
Old Bailey EC4	B43	Orme Sq. W2	A46	Pardon St. EC1	A43
Old Barrack Yd. SW1	A48	Ormonde Gte. SW3	B58	Paris Gdn. SE1	A52
Old Castle St. E1	B45	Ormonde Ter. NW8	A31	Park Clo. SW1	B48
Old Cavendish St.	**18**	Ormond Ms. WC1	A41	Park Cres. W1	A39
Old Bond St. W1	A50	Ormond Yd. SW1	A50	Park Cres. Ms. E. W1	A39
Old Broad St. EC2	B44	Orsett St. SE11	B61	Park Cres. Ms. W. W1	A39
Old Burlington St. W1	A49	Orsett Ter. W2	B36	Parkers Row SE1	B55
Oldbury Pl. W1	A39	Osbert St. SW1	B60	Parker St. WC2	B41
Old Bond St.	**19**	Osborn St. E1	B45	Parkfield St. N1	A35
Old Bond St. W1	A50	Oslo Ct. NW8	B30	Park La. W1	A48
Old Broad St. EC2	B44	Osnaburgh St. NW1	A39	Park La. W1	B49
Old Burlington St. W1	A49	Osnaburgh Ter. NW1	A39	Park Pl. SW1	B50
Oldbury Pl. W1	A39	Ossington Est. NW1	B33	Park Pl. Vill. W2	A36
Old Castle St. E1	B45	Ossulston St. NW1	A33	Park Rd. NW8	B30
Old Cavendish St.	**18**	Osten Ms. SW7	A56	Park Rd. W2	B36
Old Cavendish St. W1	B39	Oswin St. SE11	A63	Park Sq. E. NW1	A39
Old Change Ct. EC4	A53				
Old Church St. SW3	B57				

Park Sq. Ms. NW1	A39	Peter's Hl. EC4	A53	Ponsonby Ter. SW1	B60
Park Sq. W. NW1	A39	Peter's La. EC1	A43	Pont Ms. SW1	A58
Park St. SE1	A53	Peter St. W1	B40	Pont St. SW1	A58
Park St. W1	B49	Peto Pl. NW1	A39	Poplar Pl. W2	A46
Park Village E. NW1	A32	Petticoat La. E1	B45	Poppins Ct. EC4	B42
Park Village W. NW1	A32	Petty France SW1	A60	Porchester Gdns. W2	B36
Parkway NW1	A32	Petyward SW3	B57	Porchester Gdns.	B36
Park West Pl. W2	B37	Philpot La. EC3	A54	Mews W2	
Parliament Sq. SW1	B51	Phipp St. EC2	A44	Porchester Pl. W2	B37
Parliament St. SW1	B51	Phoenix Pl. WC1	A42	Porchester Rd. W2	B36
Passmore St. SW1	B58	Phoenix Rd. NW1	B33	Porchester Sq. W2	B36
Pastor St. SE11	B63	Phoenix St. WC2	B40	Porchester Ter. W2	B36
Paternoster Row EC4	B43	Piccadilly	19	Porchester Ter. N. W2	B36
Paternoster Sq. EC4	B43	Piccadilly W1	B49	Porlock St. SE1	B54
Paul St. EC2	A44	**Piccadilly Circus**	**19**	Porteus Rd. W2	A36
Paveley St. NW8	B30	Piccadilly Cir. W1	A50	Portland Pl. W1	A39
Pavilion Rd. SW1	A58	Piccadilly Pl. W1	A50	Portman Clo. W1	B38
Pavilion St. SW1	A58	Pickburn Pl. EC1	A42	Portman Ms. S. W1	B38
Peabody Av. SW1	B59	Pickering Ms. W2	B36	Portman Sq. W1	B38
Peabody Bldgs. SE1	B52	Pickle Herring St. SE1	B55	Portman St. W1	B38
Peabody Bldgs. WC1	A41	Pickwick St. SE1	B53	Portpool La. EC1	A42
Peabody Est. EC1	A43	Picton Pl. W1	B39	Portsmouth St. WC2	B41
Peabody Sq. SE1	A62	Pike Gdns. SE1	A53	Portsoken St. E1	A55
Peacock St. SE17	B63	Pilgrimage St. SE1	B54	**Portugal St.**	**24**
Pearman St. SE1	A62	**Pilgrim St.**	**25**	Portugal St. WC2	B41
Pear Tree Ct. EC1	A43	Pilgrim St. EC4	B43	Potter's Flds. SE1	B55
Pear Tree St. EC1	A43	Pilton Pl. SE17	B63	Poultry EC2	B44
Pedley St. E1	A45	Pimlico Rd. SW1	B58	Powis St. W1	A41
Pelham Ct. SW3	B57	Pindar St. EC2	A44	Praed Ms. W2	B37
Pelham Cres. SW7	B57	Pindock Ms. W9	A36	Praed St. W2	B37
Pelham Pl. SW7	B57	Pine St. EC1	A42	Pratt Wk. SE11	A61
Pelham Pl. SW7	A57	Pit Head Ms. W1	B49	Prescot St. E1	A55
Pelham St. SW7	A57	Platina St. EC2	A44	Price's St. SE1	B53
Pembroke Clo. SW1	B49	Platt St. NW1	A33	Price's Yd N1	A35
Penfold Pl. NW1	A37	Playhouse Yd. EC4	B43	Prideaux Pl. WC1	B35
Penfold St. NW8	A37	Pleasant Row NW1	A32	Primrose Hl. EC4	B42
Penrhyn St. NW1	A33	Plender Pl. NW1	A33	Primrose Hill Bridge	A31
Penrose St. SE17	B63	Plender St. NW1	A33	NW8	
Penton Pl. SE17	B63	Plough Pl. EC4	B42	Primrose St. EC2	A44
Penton Ri. WC1	B35	Plough Yd. EC2	A45	Prince Albert Rd. NW1	A31
Penton St. N1	A35	Plumtree Ct. EC4	B42	Prince Albert Rd. NW8	B30
Pentonville Rd. N1	B34	Plympton St. NW8	A37	Prince Consort Rd.	A56
Pepys St. EC3	A55	Pocock St. SE1	B53	SW7	
Percy Cir. WC1	B35	Poets Cor. SW1	B51	Princelet St. E1	A45
Percy Ms. W1	B40	Poland St.	19	Princess St. SE1	A63
Percy St. W1	B40	Poland St. W1	B40	Pr. Of Wales Ter. W8	B46
Percy St. W1	B40	Pollen St. W1	B39	Princes Gdns. SW7	B47
Percy St. WC1	B40	Polygon Rd. NW1	B33	Princes Gdns. Ms. SW7	A57
Perkins Rents. SW1	A60	Pond Ho. SW3	B57	Princes Gte. SW7	B47
Perrys Pl. W1	B40	Pond Pl. SW3	B57	Princes Gte. Ct. SW7	B47
Petersham La. SW7	A56	Ponsonby Pl. SW1	B60	Princes Ms. SW7	A57
Petersham Ms. SW7	A56			Princess St. SE1	A63
Petersham Pl. SW7	A56				

Princes St. EC2	B44
Prince's St. W1	B39
Princeton St. WC1	A41
Priory Grn. Est. N1	A34
Priory Wk. SW10	B56
Procter St. WC1	B41
Providence Ct. W1	B39
Pulteney Ter. N1	A35
Puma Ct. E1	A45
Purchese St. NW1	A33
Quaker St. E1	A45
Quality Ct. WC2	B42
Quebec Ms. W1	B38
Queen Annes Gte. SW1	B50
Queen Anne Mews W1	B39
Queen Anne St. W1	B39
Queen Elizabeth St. SE1	B55
Queenhithe EC4	A53
Queensborough Ter. W2	B36
Queensbury Ms. W. SW7	A56
Queensbury Pl. SW7	A56
Queensbury Way SW7	A57
Queens Gdns. SW3	B57
Queen's Gdns. W2	B36
Queen's Gte. SW7	A56
Queen's Gte. Gdns. SW7	A56
Queen's Gte. Ms. SW7	B46
Queens Gte. Pl. SW7	A56
Queens Gte. Pl. Ms. SW7	A56
Queen's Gte. Ter. SW7	A56
Queen's Gro. NW8	A30
Queen's Gro. Studios NW8	A30
Queens Ms. W2	B36
Queen Sq. WC1	A41
Queen Sq. Pl. WC1	A41
Queen's Ter. NW8	A30
Queen St. EC4	A53
Queen St. Mayfair W1	A49
Queen St. Pl. EC4	A53
Queen's Wk. SW1	B49
Queensway W2	B36
Queen Victoria St. EC4	A53
Quilp St. SE1	B53
Radnor Ms. W2	B37
Radnor Pl. W2	B37
Radnor Wk. SW3	B57
Railway App. SE1	B54
Railway Pl. EC3	A55
Railway St. N1	A34
Rainsford St. W2	B37
Ralph St. SE1	A63
Ralston St. SW3	B58
Ramillies Pl. W1	B40
Ramillies St.	**19**
Ramillies St. W1	B40
Rampayne St. SW1	B60
Randall Rd. SE11	B61
Randall Row SE11	B61
Randolph Cres. W9	A36
Randolph Ms. W9	A36
Randolph Rd. W9	A36
Ranelagh Bri. W2	A36
Ranelagh St. SW1	B60
Ranger St. EC3	A55
Ranston St. NW1	A37
Raphael St. SW7	B48
Rathbone Pl.	**20**
Rathbone Pl. W1	B40
Rathbone St. W1	B40
Ravent Rd. SE11	B61
Ravey St. EC2	A44
Rawlings St. SW3	B58
Raymond Bldgs. WC1	A42
Ray St. EC1	A42
Redan Pl. W2	B36
Redchurch St. E2	A45
Redcliffe Gdns. SW10	B56
Redcliffe Ms. SW10	B56
Redcliffe Rd. SW10	B56
Redcliffe Sq. SW10	B56
Redcross St. SE1	B53
Redcross Way SE1	B53
Redhill St. NW1	B32
Red Lion Ct. EC4	B42
Red Lion Sq. WC1	A41
Red Lion St. WC1	A41
Red Pl. W1	B38
Reece Ms. SW7	A57
Reedworth St. SE11	B62
Reeves Ms. W1	A48
Regal La. NW1	A32
Regency Pl. SW1	B60
Regency St. SW1	B60
Regent Pl. W1	A50
Regents Pk. Est. NW1	B32
Regent Sq. WC1	B34
Regent St.	**19**
Regent St. W1	B39
Remnant St. WC2	B41
Renfrew Rd. SE11	B62
Rennie St. SE1	A52
Reston Pl. SW7	B46
Rex Pl. W1	A49
Richard's Pl. SW3	A57
Richard Ter. Ms. SW1	B51
Richbourne Ter. SW1	B51
Richmond Bldgs. W1	B40
Richmond Ter. SW1	B51
Ridgemount Gdns. WC1	A40
Ridgemount Pl. EC1	A40
Riding Ho. St. W1	B39
Ring, The W2	A47
Risborough St. SE1	B53
Risinghill St. N1	A35
Ritchie St. N1	A35
Riverside Wk. SE1	B51
Robert Clo. W9	A36
Robert St. NW1	B32
Robert St. WC2	A51
Rochester Row SW1	B60
Rochester St. SW1	A60
Rockingham Est. SE1	A63
Rockingham St. SE1	A63
Rodmarton St. W1	A38
Rodmarton St. W1	B38
Rodney Pl. SE17	B63
Rodney Rd. SE17	B63
Rodney St. N1	A35
Roger St. WC1	A41
Roland Gdns. SW7	B56
Roland Gdns. SW10	B56
Roland Way SW10	B56
Rolls Bldgs. EC4	B42
Rolls Pass. EC4	B42
Romilly St. W1	B40
Romney St. SW1	A61
Rood La. EC3	A54
Ropemaker St. EC2	A44
Rosary Gdns. SW7	B56
Roscoe St. EC1	A43
Rose All. SE1	A53
Rose & Crown Yd. SW1	B50
Rosebery Ave. EC1	A42
Rosemoor St. SW3	B58
Rose St. WC2	A51
Rosoman St. EC1	B35
Rossmore Rd. NW1	A37

Rotary St. SE1	A63	
Rotten Row SW7	B47	
Roupell St. SE1	B52	
Rovington Clo. W2	A36	
Royal Arc. SW1	A50	
Royal Av. SW3	B58	
Royal Ex. Bldgs. EC3	B44	
Royal Hospital Rd. SW3	B58	
Royal Mint St. E1	A55	
Royal St. SE1	A62	
Rugby St. WC1	A41	
Rupert St.	**20**	
Rupert St. W1	A50	
Rushworth St. SE1	B53	
Russell Ct. SW1	B50	
Russell Pl. SW1	B60	
Russell Sq. WC1	A41	
Russell St.	**21**	
Russell St. WC2	A51	
Russia Row EC2	B43	
Rutherford St. SW1	A60	
Rutland Gte. SW7	B47	
Rutland Gte. Ms. SW7	B47	
Rutland Ms. SW7	A57	
Rutland St. SW7	A57	
Ryder St. SW1	A50	
Rysbrack St. SW3	A58	
Sackville St.	**19**	
Sackville St. W1	A50	
Saffron Hl. EC1	A42	
Sail St. SE11	A62	
St. Alban's Gro. W8	B53	
St. Albans Ms. W2	A37	
St. Albans Pl. N1	A35	
St. Albans St. SW1	A50	
St. Alphages Gdns. EC2	B43	
St. Andrews Hl. EC4	A53	
St. Andrew's Pl. NW1	B32	
St. Andrew St. EC4	B42	
St. Annes Ct. W1	A40	
St. Anns La. SW1	A60	
St. Ann's St. SW1	A60	
St. Ann's Ter. NW8	A30	
St. Anselms Pl. W1	B39	
St. Barnabas St. SW1	B59	
St. Botolph St. EC3	B45	
St. Bride St.	**25**	
St. Bride St. EC4	B42	
St. Chads Pl. WC1	B34	
St. Chads St. WC1	B34	
St. Charlotte St. W1	A40	
St. Christopher Pl. W1	B39	
St. Clare St. EC3	B45	
St. Clements La. WC2	B42	
St. Cross St. EC1	A42	
St. Dunstans Hl. EC3	A54	
St. Dunstan's La. EC3	A54	
St. Edmund's Clo. NW8	A31	
St. Edmund's Ter. NW8	A31	
St. Georges Cir. SE1	A62	
St. Georges Ct. SW7	A56	
St. Georges Dr. SW1	B59	
St. Georges Flds. W2	B37	
St. Georges Rd. SE1	A62	
St. Georges Sq. SW1	B60	
St. Georges Sq. Ms. SW1	B60	
St. George St.	**18**	
St. George St. W1	B38	
St. George St. W1	B39	
St. Giles Circus	**20**	
St. Giles Ct. WC2	B41	
St. Giles High St.	**20**	
St. Giles High St. WC2	B40	
St. Helena St. WC1	B35	
St. Helens Pl. EC3	B44	
St. James's Mkt. SW1	A50	
St. James's Pl. SW1	B50	
St. James's Row EC1	A42	
St. James's Sq.	**22**	
St. James's Sq. SW1	A50	
St. James's St. SW1	A50	
St. James's Ter. Ms. NW8	A31	
St. James's Wk. EC1	A42	
St. Johns Est. SE1	B55	
St. John's Gate EC1	A43	
St. John's La. EC1	A43	
St. John's Sq. EC1	A43	
St. Johns St. EC1	B35	
St. John's Wood Ct. NW8	A30	
St. John's Wood High St. NW8	A30	
St. John's Wood Pk NW8	A30	
St. John's Wood Rd. NW8	B30	
St. John's Wood Ter. NW8	A30	
St. Katherine's Way E1	B55	
St. Leonards Ter. SW3	B58	
St. Luke's St. SW3	B57	
St. Margarets Pl. SW1	A60	
St. Margarets St. SW1	B51	
St. Marks Sq. NW1	A32	
St. Mark St. E1	B45	
St. Martin's Ct. WC2	A51	
St. Martin's La.	**20**	
St. Martin's La. WC2	A51	
St. Martin's Le Grand EC1	B43	
St. Martin's Ms. WC2	A51	
St. Martin's Pl. WC2	A51	
St. Martin's St. WC2	A50	
St. Mary At Hl. EC3	A54	
St. Mary Axe. EC3	B44	
St. Mary's Gdns. SE11	B62	
St. Mary's Mans. W2	A36	
St. Mary's Ter. W2	A36	
St. Mary's Wk. SE11	B62	
St. Matthew St. SW1	A60	
St. Michael's St. W2	B37	
St. Olaves Ct. EC2	B44	
St. Olave's Est. SE1	B55	
St. Oswald's Pl. SE11	B61	
St. Oswulf St. SW1	B60	
St. Pancras Way NW1	A33	
St. Paul's Church Yd. EC4	B43	
St. Stephens Clo. NW8	A30	
St. Swithin's La. EC4	A54	
St. Thomas St. SE1	B54	
St. Vincent St. W1	B39	
Salamanca Pl. SE11	B61	
Salamanca St. SE11	B61	
Salem Rd. W2	B36	
Sale Pl. W2	B37	
Salisbury Ct. EC4	B42	
Salisbury Pl. W1	A38	
Salisbury Sq.	**25**	
Salisbury Sq. EC4	B42	
Salisbury St. NW8	A37	
Samford St. NW8	A37	
Sanctuary SW1	B51	
Sanctuary St. SE1	B53	
Sanctuary, The SW1	A60	
Sandcroft St. SE11	B62	
Sandell St. SE1	B52	
Sandland St. WC1	B41	

Sandwich St. WC1	B34	
Sandys Row E1	B45	
Sans Wk. EC1	A42	
Sardinia St. WC2	B62	
Saunders St. SE11	B62	
Savage Gdns. EC3	A55	
Saville Row	**19**	
Saville Row W1	A49	
Savoy Ct. WC2	A51	
Savoy Hl. WC2	A51	
Savoy Pl. WC2	A51	
Savoy St.	**21**	
Sawyer St. SE1	B53	
Scala St. W1	A40	
Scarborough St. E1	A55	
Sclater St. E1	A45	
Scoresby St. SE1	B53	
Scrutton Pl. EC2	A44	
Scrutton St. EC2	A44	
Seacoal La. EC4	B43	
Seaford St. WC1	B34	
Seaforth Pl. SW1	A60	
Seaton Pl. NW1	B32	
Secker St. SE1	B52	
Sedding St. SW1	B58	
Sedley Pl. W1	A40	
Seething La. EC3	A55	
Sekforde St. EC1	A43	
Sellon Ms. SE11	B61	
Selous St. NW1	A33	
Selwood Pl. SW7	B57	
Selwood Ter. SW7	B57	
Semley Pl. SW1	B59	
Senior St. W2	A36	
Serle St.	**24**	
Serle St. WC2	B42	
Serpentine Rd. W2	B47	
Seven Dials	**20**	
Seven Dials WC2	B41	
Seville St. SW1	B48	
Seymour Ms. W1	B38	
Seymour Pl. W1	A38	
Seymour St. W1	B38	
Seymour St. W2	B38	
Shad Thames SE1	B55	
Shaftesbury Av.	**20**	
Shaftesbury Av. W1	A50	
Shaftesbury Ct. EC3	B44	
Shafto Ms. SW1	A58	
Shand St. SE1	B54	
Shawfield St. SW3	B57	
Sheba St. E1	A45	
Sheffield St. WC2	B41	
Shelton St.	**21**	
Shelton St. WC2	B41	
Shepherd Mkt. W1	B49	
Shepherds Pl. W1	A48	
Shepherd St. W1	B49	
Sheraton St. W1	B40	
Sherborne La. EC4	A54	
Sherlock Ms. W1	A38	
Sherwood St. W1	A50	
Shoe La.	**25**	
Shoe La. EC4	B42	
Shoreditch High St. E1	A45	
Shorts Gdns.	**21**	
Shorts Gdns. WC2	B41	
Shouldham St. W1	B38	
Shroton St. NW1	A37	
Shuttle St. E1	A45	
Sicilian Av. WC1	B41	
Siddons La. NW1	A38	
Sidford Pl. SE1	A62	
Sidmouth St. WC1	B34	
Silex St. SE1	B53	
Silk St. EC2	A44	
Silver Pl. W1	B40	
Silvester St. SE1	B54	
Skin Mkt. Pl. SE1	A53	
Skinners La. EC4	A53	
Skinner St. EC1	B35	
Skipton St. SE1	A63	
Slingsby Pl. WC2	B41	
Sloane Av. SW3	B57	
Sloane Ct. E SW3	B58	
Sloane Ct. W. SW3	B58	
Sloane Gdns. SW1	B58	
Sloane Sq. SW1	B58	
Sloane St. SW1	B48	
Sloane Ter. SW1	A58	
Smallbrook Ms. W2	B37	
Smarts Pl. WC2	B41	
Smithfield St. EC1	B43	
Smith Sq. SW1	A61	
Smith St. SW3	B58	
Smith Ter. SW3	B58	
Snowdon St. EC2	A44	
Snow Hl. EC1	B43	
Snows Flds. SE1	B54	
Soho Sq.	**20**	
Soho Sq. W1	B40	
Soho St. W1	B40	
Soley Mews WC1	B35	
Somers Cres. W2	B37	
Somers Ms. W2	B37	
Southall Pl. SE1	B54	
Southampton Bldgs. WC2	B42	
Southampton Pl. WC1	B41	
Southampton Row WC1	A41	
Southampton St.	**21**	
Southampton St. WC2	A51	
South Audley St. W1	A49	
South Bolton Gdns. SW10	B56	
South Cres. WC1	A40	
South Eaton Pl. SW1	A58	
South End W8	A56	
South End Row W10	A56	
Southern St, N1	A34	
South La. NW8	B30	
South Molton La. W1	B39	
South Molton St. W1	B39	
South Molton St.	**18**	
South Pde. SW7	B57	
South Pl. EC2	B44	
South Sq. WC1	B42	
South St. W1	A49	
South Tenter St. E1	A55	
South Ter. SW7	A57	
Southwark Bri Rd. SE1	A63	
Southwark Grn. SE1	B53	
Southwark St. SE1	A53	
Southwell Gdns. SW7	A56	
South Wharf Rd. W2	B37	
Southwick Ms. W2	B37	
Southwick Pl. W2	B37	
Southwick St. W2	B37	
Spa. Grn. Est. EC1	B35	
Spanish Pl. W1	B39	
Spelman St. E1	A45	
Spencer Pl. SW1	A60	
Spenser St. SW1	A60	
Spital Sq. E1	A45	
Spital St. E1	A45	
Sprimont Pl. SW3	B58	
Spring Gdns. SW1	A50	
Spring St. W2	B37	
Stables Way SE11	B62	
Stableyard Rd. SW1	B50	

Name	Ref	Name	Ref	Name	Ref
Stable Yd. SW1	B50	Strand WC2	A51	Tabernacle St. EC2	A44
Stacey St. WC2	B41	Strand La. WC2	A52	Tachbrook Est. SW1	B60
Stackhouse St. SW3	B48	Stratford Pl. W1	B39	Tachbrook Ms. SW1	B60
Stafford Cripps Est. EC1	A43	Strathearn Pl. W2	B37	Tachbrook St. SW1	B60
Stafford Pl. SW1	A59	Stratton St. W1	A49	Talbot Sq. W2	B37
Stafford St. W1	A49	Streatham St. WC1	B41	Talbot Yd. SE1	B54
Stag Pl. SW1	A59	Strutton Ground SW1	A60	Tallis St. EC4	A52
Stainer St. SE1	B54	Strype St. E1	B45	Tanfield Ct. EC4	B42
Staining La. EC2	B43	Stukeley St. WC2	B41	Tankerton St. WC1	B34
Stalbridge St. NW1	A37	Sturge St. SE1	B53	Tanner St. SE1	B55
Stamford St. SE1	B52	Sudrey St. SE1	B53	Tanswell St. SE1	B52
Stanford Rd. W8	A56	Suffield Rd. SE17	B63	Tarver Rd. SE17	B63
Stanford St. SW1	B60	Suffolk La. EC4	A54	Taunton Ms. NW1	A38
Stanhope Bldgs. SE1	B53	Suffolk Pl. SW1	A50	Taunton Pl. NW1	A38
Stanhope Gdns. SW7	A56	Suffolk St. SW1	A50	Tavistock Pl. WC1	A41
Stanhope Gte. W1	B49	Summers St. EC1	A42	Tavistock Sq. WC1	A33
Stanhope Ms. E. SW7	A56	Sumner Bldgs. SE1	B53	Tavistock St. WC2	A51
Stanhope Ms. S. SW7	A56	Sumner Pl. SW7	B57	Taviton St. WC1	B33
Stanhope Ms. W. SW7	A56	Sumner Pl. Ms. SW7	B57	Tedworth Sq. SW3	B58
Stanhope Pl. W2	B38	Sumner St. SE1	B53	Telegraph St. EC2	B44
Stanhope Row W1	B49	Sun St. Pass. EC2	A44	**Temple Av.**	**25**
Stanhope St. NW1	B32	Sun St. Pass. EC2	B44	Temple Av. EC4	A52
Stanhope Ter. W2	A47	Surrey Row SE1	B53	Temple La. EC4	A52
Stanley Pass. NW1	A34	**Surrey St.**	**24**	**Temple Pl.**	**24**
Stanmore Pl. NW1	A32	Surrey St. WC2	A52	Temple Pl. WC2	A52
Staple Inn WC2	B42	Sussex Gdns. W2	B37	Tenison St. W1	A52
Staple Inn Bldgs. WC2	B42	Sussex Ms. W2	B37	Tenison Way SE1	B52
Starcross St. NW1	B33	Sussex Ms. W. W2	B37	Tenniel Ct. W2	B36
Star St. W2	B37	Sussex Pl. W2	B37	Tennis St. SE1	B54
Star Yd. WC2	B42	Sussex Sq. W2	B37	Tenterden St. W1	B39
Station Forecourt NW1	B33	Sussex St. SW1	B59	Tenter Gro. E1	B45
Steedman St. SE17	B63	Sutherland Row SW1	B59	Tenter St. EC2	B44
Stephenson Way NW1	B33	Sutherland St. SW1	B59	Terminus Pl. SW1	A59
Stephen St. W1	B40	Sutton Dws. SW3	B57	Tetbury Pl. N1	A35
Sterling St. SW7	B47	**Sutton Row**	**20**	Thackeray St. W8	B46
Sterry St. SE1	B54	Sutton Row W1	B40	Thanet St. WC1	B34
Steward St. E1	A45	Swallow Pl. W1	B39	Thayer St. W1	B39
Stewart's Gro. SW3	B57	Swallow St. W1	A50	Theberton St. N1	A35
Stillington St. SW1	A60	Swan Ct. SW3	B57	Theed St. SE1	B52
Stockleigh Hall NW8	A31	Swanfield St. E2	A45	Theobald's Rd. WC1	A41
Stone Bldgs. WC2	B42	Swan La. EC4	A54	Theobald's Rd. WC1	A42
Stonecutter St. EC4	B42	Swan St. SE1	A63	Thirleby Rd. SW1	A60
Stonefield St. N1	A35	Swinton Pl. WC1	B34	Thistle Gro. SW10	B56
Stones End St. SE1	A63	Swinton St. WC1	B34	Thomas Doyle St. SE1	A63
Stoney La. EC3	B45	Sydney Clo. SW7	B57	Thomas Moore St. E1	A55
Stoney St. SE1	A54	Sydney Ms. SW7	B57	Thorney St. SW1	A61
Store St. WC1	A40	Sydney Pl. SW7	B57	Thornhaugh St. WC1	A41
Storeys Gte. SW1	B50	Sydney St. SW3	B57	Thornton Pl. W1	A38
Stourcliffe St. W1	B38	Symes Ms. NW1	A33	Thorpe St. E1	B45
Strand	**21**	Symons St. SW1	B58	Thrale St. SE1	B53
		Tabard St. SE1	B54	Thrawl St. E1	B45

Walkers Ct. W1   B40
Walnut Tree Wk. SE11   A62
Walpole St. SW3   B58
Walton Pl. SW3   A58
Walton St. SW3   A57
Walworth Rd. SE17   B63
Wansey St. SE17   B63
Wardens Grn. SE1   B53
Wardour Ms. W1   B40
Wardour St.   19
Wardour St. W1   B40
Wardour St. W1   A50
Warner St. EC1   A42
Warren St. W1   A39
Warrington Cres. W9   A36
Warwick Av. W9   A36
Warwick Ct. WC1   B42
Warwick Cres. W2   A36
Warwick Est. W2   A36
Warwick Ho. St. SW1   A50
Warwick La. EC4   B43
Warwick Pl. SW1   B59
Warwick Pl. W9   A36
Warwick Row SW1   A49
Warwick Sq. EC4   B43
Warwick Sq. SW1   B59
Warwick Sq. Ms. SW1   B59
Warwick St. W1   A50
Warwick Way SW1   B59
Watergate EC4   B43
Watergate Wk. WC2   A51
Waterloo Bri.   24
Waterloo Pl.   22
Waterloo Pl. SW1   A50
Waterloo Rd. SE1   A52
Water St. WC2   A52
Watling St. EC4   B43
Waverley Pl. NW8   A30
Waverton St. W1   A49
Weavers La. SE1   B55
Weaver St. E1   A45
Webber Row SE1   B52
Webber St. SE1   B52
Weighho St. W1   B39
Weirs Pass. NW1   B33
Welbeck St.   18
Welbeck St. W1   B39
Welbeck Way W1   B39
Wellers Cres. NW1   A34

Weller St. SE1   B53
Wellington Arch W1   B49
Wellington Ct. NW8   A30
Wellington Pl. NW8   B30
Wellington Rd. NW8   A30
Wellington Sq. SW3   B58
Wellington St.   21
Wellington St. WC2   A51
Wells Ms. W1   B40
Wells Ri. NW8   A31
Wells St.   19
Wells St. W1   B40
Welsey Clo. SE17   B63
Wenworth St. E1   B45
Werrington St. NW1   A33
Wesley St. W1   B39
Westbourne Bri. W2   A36
Westbourne Cres. W2   B37
Westbourne Gdns. W2   B36
Westbourne Gro. Ter. W2   B36
Westbourne Ms. W2   B36
Westbourne Pk. Ms. W2   B36
Westbourne St. W2   B37
Westbourne Ter. W2   B36
Westbourne Ter. Rd. W2   A36
West Central Pl. WC1   B41
West Eaton Pl. SW1   A58
Westgate Ter. SW10   B56
West Halkin St. SW1   A58
West Harding St. EC4   B42
Westminster Bri. Rd. SE1   B52
Westmoreland Bldgs. EC1   B43
Westmoreland Pl. SW1   B59
Westmoreland St. W1   A39
Westmoreland Ter. SW1   B59
Weston Ri. WC1   B35
Weston St. SE1   B54
West Poultry Av. EC1   B43
West Smithfield EC1   B43
West Sq. SE11   A62
West St.   20
West St. EC2   B44
West St. WC2   B41
West Tenter St. E1   B45

West Warwick Pl. SW1   B59
Wetherby Gdns. SW5   B56
Wetherby Ms. SW5   B56
Wetherby Pl. SW7   B56
Weymouth Ms. W1   A39
Weymouth St. W1   A39
Wharfdale Rd. N1   A34
Wharf Rd. NW1   A34
Wharfside SC4   A34
Wharton St. WC1   B35
Wheat St. W1   A39
Wheler St. E1   A45
Whetstone Pk. WC2   B41
Whidborne St. WC1   B34
Whiskin St. EC1   B35
Whitby St. E1   A45
Whitcomb St.   22
Whitcomb St. WC2   A50
Whitechapel High St. E1   B45
Whitechapel Rd. E1   B45
White Church La. E1   B45
White Conduit St. N1   A35
Whitecross Pl. EC2   A44
Whitecross St. EC1   A43
Whitefriars St. EC4   B42
Whitehall   23
Whitehall SW1   B51
Whitehall Ct.   23
Whitehall Ct. SW1   B51
Whitehall Gdns. SW1   B51
Whitehall Pl.   23
Whitehall Pl. SW1   B51
White Hart St. SE11   B54
White Hart Yd. SE1   B54
Whitehaven St. NW8   A37
Whiteheads Gro. SW3   B57
Whitehorse St. W1   B49
White Kennet St. E1   B45
White Lion St. N1   A35
Whites Grounds SE1   B54
White's Grounds Est. SE1   B54
White's Row E1   B45
Whitfield Pl. W1   A40
Whitfield St. W1   A40
Whitgift St. SE11   B61
Whittaker St. SW1   B58
Whittlesey St. SE1   B52
Wickham St. SE11   B61

Wicklow St. WC1	B34
Wide Gates E1	B45
Wigmore Pl. W1	B39
Wigmore St.	**18**
Wigmore St. W1	B38
Wilbraham Pl. SW1	A58
Wild Ct. WC2	B41
Wild St. WC2	B41
Wilfred St. SW1	A60
William Ms. SW1	B48
William Rd. NW1	B32
William St. SW1	B48
William St. EC2	B44
William IV St. WC2	A51
William IV St.	**21**
Willow Pl. SW1	A60
Willow St. EC2	A44
Willy St. WC1	B41
Wilmington Sq. WC1	B35
Wilmington St. WC1	B35
Wilson St. EC2	B44
Wilton Cres. SW1	B48
Wilton Ms. SW1	A59
Wilton Pl. SW1	B48
Wilton Rd. SW1	A59
Wilton Row SW1	B48
Wilton St. SW1	A59
Wilton Ter. SW1	B58
Wiltshire Clo. SW3	B58
Wimpole Ms. W1	A39

Wimpole St.	**18**
Wimpole St. W1	A39
Winchester Clo. SE17	B63
Winchester Sq. SE1	A54
Winchester St. SE1	A54
Winchester St. SW1	B59
Winchester Wk. SE1	B54
Wincott St. SE11	B62
Windmill St.	**20**
Windmill St. W1	B40
Windmill St. W1	A50
Windmill Wk. SE1	B52
Windsor Pl. SW1	A60
Wine Office Ct.	**25**
Wine Office Ct. EC4	B42
Winsland Ms. W2	B37
Winsland St. W2	B37
Winsley St. W1	B40
Withers Pl. EC1	A43
Woburn Pl. WC1	A41
Woburn Sq. WC1	A40
Woburn Wk. WC1	B33
Wolseley Pl. SE1	B55
Woodbridge St. EC1	A42
Woodfall St. SW3	B58
Woodseer St. E1	A45
Woods Ms. W1	A48
Woodstock Ms. W1	A39
Woodstock St. W1	B39

Wood St. EC2	B43
Wootton St. SE1	B52
Worgan St. SE11	B61
Wormwood St. EC2	B44
Woronzow Rd. NW8	A30
Worship St. EC2	A44
Wren St. WC1	A42
Wyndham Ms. W1	A38
Wyndham Pl. W1	A38
Wyndham St. W1	A38
Wynford Rd. N1	A35
Wynyard Ter. SE11	B62
Wythburn Pl. W1	B38
Yardley St. WC1	B35
Yarmouth Pl. W1	B49
Yeomans Row SW3	A57
York Bridge NW1	A38
York Bldgs. WC2	A51
York Gte. NW1	A39
York Pl. WC2	A51
York Rd. SE1	B51
York St. W1	A38
York Ter. E. NW1	A39
York Ter. W. NW1	A38
York Way N1	A34
York Way Ct. N1	A34
Young St. W8	B46

NOTES